AROUND L(
THE GUID

Published in 2010
by
Aird Trading, Aird House, Aird of Sleat,
Isle of Skye. IV45 8RN.
Author: Lynne Woods
Assistant Editor: Doug Vickers
Field Assistant: Lance Jackson

ISBN 978-0-9562126-1-0

Printed by Mayoh Press Ltd.
www.mayohpress.com

Cover picture: Urquhart Castle & Loch Ness by Grumpy George
www.grumpygeorge.co.uk

INTRODUCTION

Welcome to "Around Loch Ness: The Guide Book," another in the series "See it...Do it....Don't miss it." The aim of each of these books is to help visitors to do just that, to make the most of their stay in a given area. It would be impossible to list everything of interest or name every individual shop, hotel, gallery, craft outlet etc. but what is hoped is that by taking you around an area, including "off the beaten track," you will have the pleasure of discovering for yourself many of the additional delights which it was not possible to include here.

The book is divided into sections, arranged in a logical order for touring either part or all of the area around Loch Ness. The map on page 7 identifies each of these sections. The numbers on the map correspond with the numbered sections of the book. Please note that the maps are not intended for precise navigation; their purpose is to illustrate the general location of things mentioned in the text.

Inside the back cover you will find a list of relevant Ordnance Survey maps. There is also a list of useful telephone numbers. Public toilets are listed in red at the end of sections where appropriate. Some internet access points are listed but it is not possible to provide a comprehensive list.

Whilst every attempt has been made to ensure accuracy, things do change with the creation of new enterprises and the disappearance of businesses as people retire or move on, a fact for which the publishers cannot accept responsibility.

You will notice that in this part of the World many names have more than one spelling and there is often more than one place with the same name. It all adds to the interest!

It is hoped that this guide book will enable you to discover some of the less well advertised delights of this beautiful and fascinating part of Scotland and that you will use it again and again on return visits.

CONTENTS

AROUND LOCH NESS : AN INTRODUCTION

Think of Loch Ness and it is impossible not to wonder about its famous, albeit doubtful, inhabitant - the Loch Ness Monster. However, in an area of such diversity there is so much more to discover: The western side is renowned for attractions to satisfy monster fans but away from the busy A82 are quiet back roads leading to beautiful, tranquil places. The eastern side of the loch is remote, untamed and timeless. Although less well known, it has a wealth of beauty and history to discover. Beyond Loch Ness, to the south lie the other lochs which fill the Great Glen and to the north are Inverness and the Beauly and Moray Firths.

Loch Ness: The Classic View

Loch Ness

Loch Ness stretches 23 miles from Fort Augustus in the south almost to Inverness in the north. In places it is 330 metres deep, holding more fresh water than any other lake or loch in the British Isles. It has never been known to freeze. The journey around the loch can be travelled almost entirely next to the shore, from which the walls of the Great Glen rise steeply through mixed woodland, moors and peat bogs to majestic craggy peaks. Loch Ness has long been considered a place of great mystery because of the alleged existence of a "monster." (St. Columba was one of the first recorded "Nessie-spotters!") While many reports have later proved to have been hoaxes, there remain unexplained sightings and scientific investigation has proved inconclusive.

More reliable than the monster are the salmon which return each year to spawn in Loch Ness. Other fish include char, eel, several different types of trout and the caviar-bearing sturgeon. There are also pike, minnow and stickleback. A variety of birdlife fish on the loch, including the elusive Osprey which return to the area each year.

The Great Glen

The Great Glen, also called Glen Mor, is the massive 380 million year old fault line which runs more than sixty miles diagonally across Scotland. Between great mountain ranges, four lochs fill much of this rift valley which was left behind after huge geological upheaval. Of these, Loch Ness is the largest: The others are Lochs Lochy, Oich and Dochfour. The Great Glen between Fort William and Inverness has become a popular long-distance hiking route of over 70 miles, a third of which runs beside the

The Great Glen

Caledonian Canal. A similar route exists for cyclists but it is also a wonderful place to explore by car with many side roads and innumerable views to discover.

The Caledonian Canal

The Caledonian Canal, strictly speaking, is not one canal but four major feats of engineering. Of its total length of over sixty miles only twenty-two are artificial waterway. The remaining sections are the four freshwater lochs which the canal links together to provide a continuous waterway from Corpach, near Fort William, to the Beauly Firth at Inverness. The canal includes twenty-nine locks, ten bridges and four aqueducts.

The Caledonian Canal

British Waterways have owned the canal since 1962 and have gradually been repairing and refurbishing it. It is now busier than ever with many pleasurecaft passing through its waters each year.

The canal was built for two reasons; firstly, to provide an alternative route for sailing ships instead of mariners having to brave the stormy seas around the top of Scotland. Secondly, the canal was to provide employment at a time when many Highlanders were destitute. Designed by Thomas Telford, the canal was begun in 1803 before the existence of huge earth moving machinery so had to be dug by hand. The canal took much longer to build than expected, in spite of being dug from both ends. It was to have bigger locks than previously seen as well as many innovations which, for the time, were quite revolutionary. These included low level swing bridges instead of bridges which lifted up. Even the use of wheelbarrows was fairly novel in those days!

By the time the canal was completed in 1822, steam was replacing sail and it never did become the busy industrial waterway which had been intended. Over nearly two centuries it has had a chequered history but is recognised as one of Scotland's iconic engineering feats - to such an extent that it now enjoys Scheduled Ancient Monument status.

Thomas Telford

Thomas Telford was born in Dumfriesshire in 1757. His father died when he was young and a relative paid for Thomas to train as a stonemason. He moved around the country, including such places as London and Portsmouth, to gain experience. He was appointed Surveyor, Engineer and Architect to the Ellesmere Port Canal Company and subsequently as Chief Engineer for the Shrewsbury Canal. He went on to build the Crinan Canal and then the Caledonian Canal, which took nineteen years to complete, twelve years longer than anticipated. The cost was not much less than a million pounds. It finally opened in 1822. As well as canals, Telford also built countless roads and bridges. When he died in 1834 he was buried in Westminster Abbey as a mark of respect for his achievements.

The People

Evidence of habitation around Loch Ness stretches back through the mists of time, probably less people living here now than at some other times during its long and lively history. Remains from The Stone Age as well as remnants of Bronze and Iron Age forts can still be seen. Pictish tribes settled here, Inverness being the capital of their kingdom, before Celts arrived from Ireland with Christian missionary saints, including St. Ninian and St. Columba. Family clans developed and for many centuries this system was the dominant social structure. Loyalties were put to the test during the Jacobite uprisings, culminating in the Battle of Culloden in 1746.

Much of the Clan system was destroyed during the notorious "Clearances" of the eighteenth and nineteenth centuries when Highlanders were evicted in order for the land to be turned over to the more profitable sheep grazing. Chiefs became mere landlords, rather than leaders and paternal figures. Eventually, resentment and rebellion brought about the introduction of the Crofting Laws and crofters were allowed to own their own land. This system endures today with many crofters running small holdings in parallel with other employment.

The Wildlife

The varied terrain around Loch Ness provides habitats for a huge variety of wildlife. Three types of deer (red, roe and sika) live here, along with badgers, foxes, otters, mountain hares and pine marten. Red squirrels, smaller than their grey counterparts, still thrive here. Grouse and other wildfowl roam the moors; water birds frequent the lochs; buzzards, red kites and golden eagles soar amongst the mountains.

Bonny Prince Charlie

The area is rich in tales of Charles Edward Stewart's escapades in his unsuccessful attempts to claim the Scottish throne. Innumerable legends tell of narrow escapes as the Redcoats approached. There are monuments to look-alike followers, slain whilst acting as decoys, and rocks which still bear the marks where Jacobite swords were sharpened. At Culloden, east of Inverness, he was finally defeated by the

Red deer

army of King George II. After the Prince escaped to France he lived another forty years as guest of various European courts but without his own throne. He took to drink, his wife deserted him to live in a convent and it was left to his daughter Charlotte to nurse him in his decline.

Something for everyone....

Around Loch Ness there is something for everyone - from Scotland's iconic canal to the grandeur of the mountains and wide open moors; from the tranquillity and beauty of the glens to the fun of the lively Nessie venues and the attractions of the modern cosmopolitan city of Inverness.

AROUND LOCH NESS

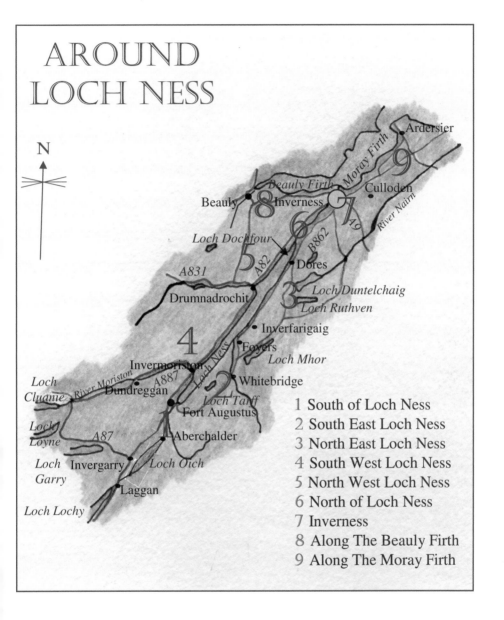

1 South of Loch Ness
2 South East Loch Ness
3 North East Loch Ness
4 South West Loch Ness
5 North West Loch Ness
6 North of Loch Ness
7 Inverness
8 Along The Beauly Firth
9 Along The Moray Firth

The numbers on this map correspond with the numbered sections of the book.

Please note: Petrol filling stations can be few and far between in some areas, especially on the eastern side of the loch where there are none between Fort Augustus and Inverness.

SOUTH OF LOCH NESS

The stretch of the Great Glen between Laggan and Fort Augustus is perhaps where it is most obvious how The Caledonian Canal links four separate lochs to form one continuous waterway: Loch Lochy is connected to the southern end of Loch Oich at Laggan. In turn, Loch Oich connects with Loch Ness via a stretch of canal culminating in a dramatic staircase of five locks at Fort Augustus. To travel the canal by boat or along the tow path is to follow a peaceful, linear route, the scenery more spectacular with each mile. Lochs Lochy and Oich are both long and narrow, the sides of the Great Glen rift valley rising steeply on either side. The stretch of canal between Aberchalder and Fort Augustus meanders peacefully through the eastern edge of Inchnacardoch Forest.

Half way along Loch Oich is Invergarry and to the west is Glen Garry, which joins Glen Moriston. The scenery is breathtaking – Glen Garry wild and dramatic, Glen Moriston sheltered and picturesque.

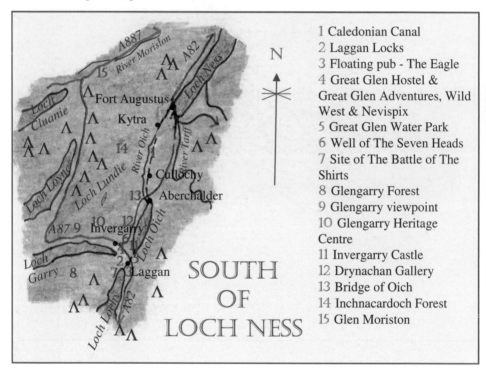

1 Caledonian Canal
2 Laggan Locks
3 Floating pub - The Eagle
4 Great Glen Hostel & Great Glen Adventures, Wild West & Nevispix
5 Great Glen Water Park
6 Well of The Seven Heads
7 Site of The Battle of The Shirts
8 Glengarry Forest
9 Glengarry viewpoint
10 Glengarry Heritage Centre
11 Invergarry Castle
12 Drynachan Gallery
13 Bridge of Oich
14 Inchnacardoch Forest
15 Glen Moriston

Laggan

At Laggan, boats leave Loch Lochy to enter a two mile stretch of the Caledonian Canal. There is a car park and **picnic site** near the locks. "The Eagle," is a Dutch barge converted to a **floating pub.** South of the locks, on the western side of Loch Lochy, is the site of **The Battle of The Shirts** which was fought in 1544 on a very hot day, hence the name of the battle - the combatants shed their heavy outer clothes and fought in their shirts.

The Eagle - a pub afloat!

The Great Glen Way follows the tow path here through "Laggan Avenue," an attractive wooded section. At North Laggan, a **swing bridge** allows boats to pass through to Loch Oich.
"Highland Activities" at **The Great Glen Water Park** is an all year round activity centre for white water rafting, canoeing, other watersports and abseiling. Booking is advisable. **The Great Glen Hostel** offers reasonably priced accommodation and is also the base of **Great Glen Adventures**. (See their website for details.) **Wild West** (opposite the Forest Lodge Guest House) offer unforgettable wildlife spotting trips for small groups. At the same location **Nevispix** run pre-booked wildlife photography safaris and workshops. West of Laggan, **Glengarry Forest** is a favourite place for seeing red squirrels.
Loch Oich
From Laggan, the A82 runs along the western side of Loch Oich through

pleasant woodland of beech, silver birch, oak, ash, rowan and mixed firs. The level of the loch can vary considerable due to the fact that its waters form part of a hydro-electric scheme. **The Great Glen Way** crosses the road at the swing bridge and between Laggan and Aberchalder continues along the quieter, eastern shore of the loch, an area known for its summer display of purple orchids.

Loch Oich

South of Invergarry, on the shores of **Loch Oich,** is **The Well of the Seven Heads** which gained its name by gruesome means: In 1663, seven members of the MacDonald Clan were slaughtered in a retribution killing and their severed heads washed in this well before being taken to the MacDonnell Chief in Invergarry

Well of The Seven Heads

9

Castle. A plaque tells the story. The monument on top of the well was erected in 1812.

Across the road from the well is the small but extremely well stocked **Seven Heads Store,** incorporating a newsagents, off-licence and general store – a good place to buy goodies to enjoy on the nearby loch-side picnic site.

Book exchange at Invergarry Post Office

A well with a gruesome history!

Invergarry is a small, attractive village situated at the junction of the A82 and the A87. An excellent centre from which to explore a wide area, it also makes a good stopping place for those going further north or west. The **Glengarry Heritage Centre,** situated in the Community Hall next to the shinty pitch, provides an informative history of Glengarry and the surrounding area. Also situated in the hall are **public toilets** and a **cafe.**

The small **post office** on the main road (A87) is an excellent source of local information. It is also the place to pick up a good read in their **book exchange** for a small donation to charity or, even better, swap a finished book you don't wish to carry any further!

There is a **filling station** just past the junction on the A87 Fort Augustus road. Invergarry is notable for the number of walks and tracks to be found in the surrounding forests. One particularly pleasant one begins in the village: From a metal gate between the two white cottages on the Skye road, a track leads up to lovely **Loch Lundie**. (A steep start but levelling off – map and boots recommended.) To walk there and back takes about an hour and a half but it is possible to extend the walk beyond the loch to the swing bridge at Aberchalder, near the historic Bridge of Oich, and back through the forest on part of the Great Glen Way. A walk along the river bank

The River Garry

begins from near the post office where a path leads down to an iron suspension bridge.

The ruins of **Invergarry Castle,** once the stronghold of the Clan Chiefs of the MacDonnells of Glengarry, are to be found in the grounds of **The Glengarry Castle Hotel.** The castle was destroyed by fire in the seventeenth century, rebuilt shortly afterwards and then partially destroyed again in 1754 by government troops. The hotel, once known as Invergarry House, was built in 1869 by the Ellice family, then lairds of Glengarry. It became the Glengarry Castle Hotel in 1960 and enjoys spectacular views over Loch Oich. It is renowned for afternoon teas but, unfortunately, is not open all year. The friendly and comfortable four star **Invergarry Hotel**, built in 1885, was once a coaching inn and is a good place to stay or call in for a meal.

In addition to hotels, there are several places in the immediate area offering hostel and lodge accommodation, also a **floating bunk house** on a barge.

The Forestry Commission land to the west of Invergarry has several **way-marked trails.** Car parking is signposted from the road.

Glen Garry.

It is possible to leave Invergarry by the A87, travel through Glen Garry and Glen Moriston and then rejoin the A82 at Invermoriston. (For Glen Moriston see section on South West Loch Ness.) About five miles west of Invergarry, a minor road branches off to follow **Loch Garry**, once a thriving part of Scotland with a substantial population but emptied of most of its inhabitants during the notorious Clearances of the eighteenth century.

Loch Garry

The road follows the shores of **Loch Garry** and then **Loch Quoich**, two lochs of special interest to bird watchers for here the rare Scoter and the Black Throated Diver can be seen. This route eventually reaches Kinloch Hourn at the head of Loch Hourn on the West coast. The road was built by Telford to serve what was then the sizeable fishing industry in Loch Hourn.

Local seafood

Six miles along this road, at the western end of Loch Garry, can be found **Tomdoun Seafood Restaurant and**

Hotel. This is yet another of Scotland's well kept secrets! The seafood is some of Scotland's finest (langoustines a speciality) and the location would be difficult to surpass anywhere in the World.

Glengarry Viewpoint by the side of the A87 provides stunning views over the loch, which viewed from here looks like a map of Scotland!

Invergarry to Fort Augustus

A mile and a half north of Invergarry, on the A82, is the **Drynachan Gallery -** Woodturning with a difference: Local, untreated, "green" wood is used to unusual effect depending on how the wood continues to age and dry after turning. A family heirloom on display in the gallery is the hundred year old treadle lathe. Woodturning courses are available here by prior arrangement. (Also B and B accommodation.)

The Bridge of Oich

The Bridge of Oich

The Bridge of Oich is a historic suspension bridge spanning the River Oich near **Aberchalder**. Designed by James Dredge, the bridge was built in 1854 and was in use until 1932. A small car park is signposted from the road.

Nearby is the swing bridge which now carries the road over the Caledonian Canal at the northern end of Loch Oich. Aberchalder is a place renowned for its home baking: **The Bridge House Tea Garden** offers "elevenses," light lunches and afternoon teas in the garden. (People actually travel here for the home made cakes!) North of Aberchalder, **The Thistle Stop** is also well worth visiting for the gift shop and cafe - but be prepared to have to make the difficult choice between home-made Bakewell Tart and the speciality Apple Pie. (Mmmm! with just a hint of spice.) Open March to the end of November.

Above Aberchalder the **Calder Burn** runs down **Glen Buck.** There are several tracks and footpaths and some **waterfalls** about three quarters of a mile from Aberchalder.

As the A82 continues to Fort Augustus, the Great Glen gradually widens to the point where Loch Ness begins. The canal towpath between Aberchalder and Fort Augustus is part of the Great Glen Way, this section making an extremely scenic, level walk. At both Cullochy and Kytra there are locks and information boards about the canal.

Inchnacardoch Forest, to the west of this section of the canal, has several way-marked trails which can be accessed from the car park near The Bridge of Oich or from the minor road south from Fort Augustus on the opposite side of the canal to the A82.

Public Toilets
Invergarry – Community Centre
Fort Augustus, main car park

2. SOUTH EAST LOCH NESS, STRATHERRICK

Although not far from either Inverness or Fort Augustus, the area to the South East of Loch Ness, known as Stratherrick, is wild, remote and hauntingly beautiful. The name, from the Gaelic "Strath Fhaireag," means "broad valley of lapwings" and is particularly appropriate in spring when they return and the area comes alive with their call. Along

Loch Mhor

the narrow band of fertile land by Loch Ness, up the steep sides of The Great Glen and on to the foothills of the majestic Monadhliath Mountains, a network of quiet, mainly single track roads traverse a surprisingly varied terrain. There are forests and moors, lochs and lochans (small lochs) and steep glens, down which rush tumbling streams. A particularly attractive feature is the number of remaining tracts of mixed woodland with mature oak and pine trees as well as beech, ash, birch, rowan, hazel and aspen.

The diverse habitats are home to many species of wild life: Otters, foxes, badgers, pine marten and red squirrels live here, as well as roe deer, red deer and sika deer. Interbreeding between the latter two species has also resulted in some very dark stags which are smaller than normal red deer. Whilst the lochs attract a wide variety of water birds, on the moors live grouse and other wild fowl including introduced pheasant and red legged partridge. Above the mountains soar birds of prey such as golden eagles, buzzards, peregrines, osprey and the rare red kite. Other visitors to the area include geese and whooper swans en route to their winter feeding grounds. Slavonian Grebes have their only Scottish breeding ground here. Also in Stratherrick, unusually for this far north, are a number of barn owls.

Humans, too, have long populated this part of the Highlands – from ancient Picts and nomadic Christian missionaries to more recent Clansmen and Jacobite rebels, all leaving behind traces of their presence.

Of great historical and natural interest, the area is also ideally suited to outdoor activities. The numerous forest tracks, many way-marked, are ideal for strolling, serious walking or mountain biking. Other opportunities include fresh water fishing, canoeing and sailing, deer stalking and horse riding. For the less energetic, it is simply a wonderful place to relax amongst superb scenery.

The River Foyers

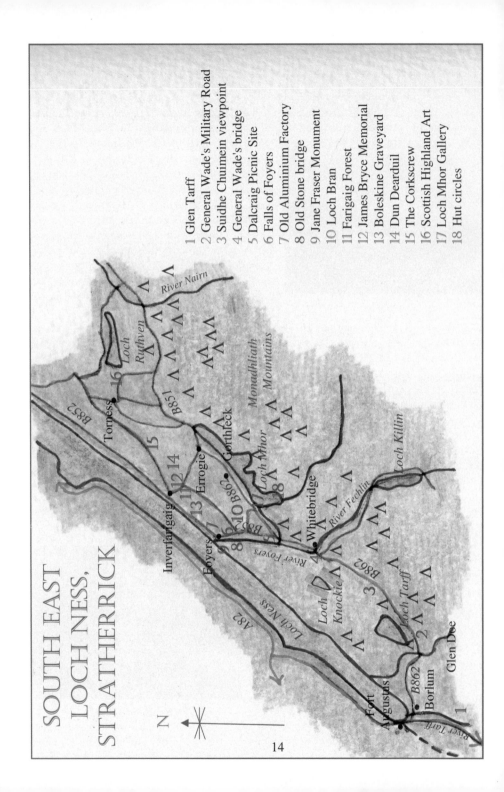

SOUTH EAST LOCH NESS, STRATHERRICK

N

1 Glen Tarff
2 General Wade's Military Road
3 Suidhe Chuimein viewpoint
4 General Wade's bridge
5 Dalcraig Picnic Site
6 Falls of Foyers
7 Old Aluminium Factory
8 Old Stone bridge
9 Jane Fraser Monument
10 Loch Bran
11 Farigaig Forest
12 James Bryce Memorial
13 Boleskine Graveyard
14 Dun Dearduil
15 The Corkscrew
16 Scottish Highland Art
17 Loch Mhor Gallery
18 Hut circles

Borlum.

Loch Ness from Borlum

East of Fort Augustus, the B862 crosses the **River Tarff** upstream from where it enters Loch Ness. **Glen Tarff**, reached along a track signposted "Ardachy Bridge," is popular with walkers. On a clear day the view up the loch from Borlum is worth pausing to enjoy.

Beyond Borlum the road follows the southern tip of the loch to climb steeply away between mixed woodland and roadside banks of ferns before crossing

Glen Doe (which is part of a huge hydro electric scheme) and emerging onto open moorland on the Glendoe Estate where deer can often be seen.

Loch Tarff (some distance from the river of the same name) is very picturesque, fringed by birch trees and home to many different water birds. The water supply for Fort Augustus comes from here. To the south are the hills of Glendoe Forest, to the north east the Monadhliath Mountains. From the most easterly corner of Loch Tarff a track follows the stream

Loch Tarff

General Wade's Military Roads

Until the eighteenth century Scotland had few proper roads. In 1724 King George I sent Major-General George Wade to see how the rebellious Highlanders could best be subdued. Wade decided a good road network was necessary for government troops to travel more quickly, the first being built between Fort William and Inverness. The present main road follows the western shore of Loch Ness but Wade's original route, completed in 1733, went east of the loch. Much of the road is single track with passing places. It does not hug the shore, as does its western counterpart the A82, but the terrain is dramatic and the views spectacular. Between 1724 and 1740 General Wade oversaw the construction of almost two hundred and fifty miles of roads and forty bridges. Ironically, the improved roads also benefitted Charles Edward Stewart (Bonnie Prince Charlie) in the second Jacobite uprising of 1745, which ended with his defeat at the bloody Battle of Culloden the following year. Wade's road network was later greatly extended by engineer Thomas Telford who also built the Caledonian Canal.

which flows out of **Dubh Lochan** high above to the south west. (This is a strenuous walk requiring suitable footwear and clothing.)

Much of the B862 follows the route of one of General Wade's military roads.

At **Suidhe Chuimein Viewpoint** the B862 reaches its highest point at 1275 feet. Gaelic for "Columba's seat," the saint is said to have rested here on his way from Iona. The view is superb. In the foreground, to the north, are **Loch Knockie** and **Loch Mhor.** To the west, **Loch Ness** is hidden from view in the huge trench that is the Great Glen. To the north east, the rift extends towards Inverness and the Moray Firth. An information board gives details. A stunning walk begins from the nearby stile and leads to a track running along the ridge almost to Loch Tarff. (It is a popular place for **red deer** so it is wise to keep dogs restrained.)

Two miles north of the viewpoint a small road leads down to pretty **Loch Knockie** and the **Knockie Lodge Hotel.**

Whitebridge takes its name from General Wade's elegant, single-arched bridge

Wade's bridge, Whitebridge

which has spanned the **River Fechlin** here since 1732. It is intact but in a poor state of repair, although there are hopes it will be restored. Each summer it is covered with lovely pink Fairy Foxglove flowers. Whitebridge is unspoilt and popular for outdoor pursuits including bird watching, deer stalking and brown trout fishing in one of three lochs on private estates. (Such activities can usually be organised by hotels.) There are several signposted **forest trails** which offer excellent routes for walkers or

The Whitebridge Hotel

mountain bikers.

Whitebridge was once the site of one of the "King's Houses" – inns built to accommodate soldiers and other travellers. General Wade would almost certainly have stayed here. The present **Whitebridge Hotel** dates from 1899 and was built on the site of a former inn which burned down. From the dining room are spectacular views towards the Monadhliath Mountains. The bar is mentioned in real ale guides but also offers an extensive range of single malt whiskies. (Tel: 01456 486226.) Self catering accommodation is available at **Wildside Lodges** next to Wade's bridge.

16

From Whitebridge an unclassified road climbs high above the **River Fechlin** with spectacular views of the rugged crags and peaks of the Monadhliath Mountains. Near Garrogie Lodge the road drops to **Loch Killin,** nestling picturesquely in the mountains, and then following the loch side (this part closed to vehicles) before coming to an end at Killin Lodge.

Loch Killin

Dalcrag Picnic site
North of the junction of the B852 with the B862 is a pleasant picnic site in birch woodland on the banks of the **River Fechlin**. Just beyond this point the River Fechlin becomes the **River Foyers**.
Foyers
Foyers is an interesting place with a long

Upper Foyers

history, there being evidence of Neolithic then Pictish settlements before a succession of early saints and other religious figures arrived. The area also has a turbulent Clan history, influence shifting from the Lairds of Moray in the eleventh and twelfth centuries to the Grants in the thirteenth century. A daughter of the Frasers later married into the Grant family. As the Grants lost land to pay debts, the Frasers became dominant and remained so until the nineteenth century when the Foyers Estate had to be sold off to pay huge debts. It changed hands a further twice before being sold to the British Aluminium Company in 1895.

Upper and Lower Foyers are separated by a deep gorge down which rushes the River Foyers. At **Upper Foyers** there is a small car park opposite the entrance to the waterfalls, some public toilets, a restaurant, public telephone, and a post office/general store which sells wines & spirits, bread, milk, newspapers etc. For licensed accommodation (bar but no restaurant) with the ultimate view of Loch Ness from the terrace, **Foyers House** is signposted from near to the post office.

The Falls of Foyers
The spectacular **Falls of Foyers** have attracted visitors since Victorian times. The Gaelic name "Eas na

The falls of Foyers

Smuid" translates as "waterfall of smoke" – probably for the spray which billows out when the River Foyers is in full spate as it plunges down between banks of heather and Scots pine to join Loch Ness. There are **Upper and Lower Falls.** The

The path to the Falls of Foyers

main entrance to The Lower Falls is opposite the post office. Here a seat and picnic table with a stunning woodland view make a delightful spot to eat al fresco. A circular walk can take in both waterfalls. For the less energetic, the viewpoint for the 80 feet drop of the Lower Falls is near the entrance. A set of information boards provides a fascinating insight into Foyers history, including details of famous visitors. These include the intrepid Boswell and Johnson as well

Robert Burns was inspired here!

as Robert Burns, who was so inspired here in 1787 that he wrote a poem on the spot! His verses appear etched on slate alongside the path. Keats and Wordsworth also visited, as well as William Topaz McGonagall, famous for being Scotland's worst poet! Viewing the falls was once fraught with danger. Nowadays, a well kept walkway leads to the viewpoint and a network of paths connect Upper and Lower Foyers.

Lower Foyers
From Upper Foyers, a woodland track (Scottish Public Right of Way) runs downhill to Lower Foyers and Loch Ness. Half way down the track, close to the

Lower Foyers

road, is a wooden bungalow called **The Turning Point** which offers simple but homely B and B. On the wall outside there is usually an informative display about local points of interest. There is also an excellent, hand drawn map entitled "The Foyers Maze" detailing all the points of interest and paths in the area. Extremely nominally priced, this is a seriously useful piece of paper and well worth seeking out. (Dogs can be assured of a bowl of water here while their human counterparts peruse the information!) The woods between Lower and Upper Foyers are home to pine marten, roe and sika deer and red squirrels.

The Old Aluminium Factory

The old aluminium factory

On the loch side is an imposing stone building, once the British Aluminium factory, built in 1896 and the first in Britain. Foyers was one of the first villages in Scotland to have its own electricity supply. Water from the River Foyers was used to generate electricity for the smelting process, the raw bauxite being transported by train from Fort William to Fort Augustus then by barge to **Foyers Pier** which was constructed by Telford. A light railway ran from the wharf to the works and the community of Lower Foyers grew up near the factory. The area was bombed during the Second World War because aluminium from here was used to make fighter planes. Aluminium has not been smelted here since 1967 and the building now houses a set of generators which supplement electricity produced by the nearby **Hydro Electric plant.** The pier, signposted from near the factory, is now used only by pleasure craft and canoeists. A public footpath runs from here along the loch side for two miles to Inverfarigaig.

The Stone Bridge

A "Bailey" bridge crosses the River at Lower Foyers. Upstream from here is a lovely old stone bridge, unfortunately closed to the public now because of its dangerous state of disrepair. A small road leads directly to this bridge from the bus stop near the houses. There is space to park near the bridge and paths are signposted to the Upper and Lower falls and Whitebridge. (3 miles.)

Loch-side walks

Loch Ness at Lower Foyers

Upper and Lower Foyers are criss-crossed with footpaths through the woods and along the shore. These can be accessed from either side of the "Bailey" bridge, from the old aluminium factory and from the graveyard. The paths down either side of the River Foyers are overhung with beech, oak and ash trees. (In September there are rich pickings here for blackberry lovers!) **Foyers Bay** is particularly pleasant with shallow water and a sandy shoreline.

The Jane Fraser Monument

From the stone bridge a lane leads to the

*Jane Fraser
Monument*

graveyard. Through an iron gate a wide, beech-lined track goes to the extremely picturesque **Foyers Old Cemetery**. At one corner, a stile opens on to the banks of the loch where a monument commemorates a sad love story: Jane Fraser was to marry her cousin, whom she loved deeply. However, on a visit to Foyers he fell out of a fruit tree and was killed. Jane went into a decline and spent her days at this spot looking across the loch to where her lover had lived. In the hope that she could learn to love anther, her parents married her to Thomas Fraser of Balnain. Sadly, she pined away and died before her first wedding anniversary. She was buried at the spot from which she had so often gazed across the loch, where the monument now stands.

The inscription reads:

*To the memory of Jane, spouse of Thomas
Fraser of Balnain. She was the only child
of Simon Fraser of Foyers and of
Elizabeth Grant his wife. She added to
superior personal Graces and Talents of
the first order the humblest piety, the
sweetest of manner and the most devoted
filial affection. Her spotless life was
closed by a tranquil and Christian death
on the 7th of July 1817 in the 22nd year of
her age.*

The Craigdarroch Hotel and **Foyers Bay House** both serve food and offer good views of the loch while dining.

From Foyers the narrow B852 runs north beside the loch. The road is lined on both sides with trees and the roadside verges are filled with wild flowers.

Boleskine Graveyard

Boleskine Graveyard

A mile or so north of Foyers is Boleskine Graveyard. One gravestone bears three marks made by musket balls in 1746 when a funeral party was attacked by redcoats. On the opposite side of the road is **Boleskine House**, built in the eighteenth century as a hunting lodge. It was later owned by Aleister Crowley, a practioner in black magic and said to be the most wicked man in Europe, and then for a while by Jimmy Page of the band Led Zeppelin.

Inverfarigaig and Farigaig Forest

Inverfarigaig, approximately half way along Loch Ness, is a small settlement in the shadow of towering, craggy peaks. Another of Telford's constructions, **Inverfarigaig Pier** is now dilapidated but a good place for expansive views of Loch Ness.

Farigaig Forest is managed by the Scottish Forestry Commission and has several **way-marked trails.**

In the car park is a small information centre, toilets and an "**outdoor classroom**" with striking **carved statues** of woodland animals. Badgers, foxes and pine marten all live in the forest and in spring woodpeckers

Woodland carvings

and cuckoos can be heard.

One path from the car park leads to **Lochan Torr an Tuill**, a picturesque lochan in the forest.

High above Inverfarigaig is **Dun Dearduil,** the remains of an Iron Age fort, reputedly home of Deirdre of The Sorrows, an Irish princess who had the misfortune to fall in love with

Farigaig Forest

someone from a rival family. ("Dearduil" is the Gaelic form of "Deirdre.")

Three roads leave Inverfarigaig, the "main" one being the B852 which follows the shores of Loch Ness between Foyers and Inverness. However, to follow this road without detouring would be to miss some of Scotland's most spectacular scenery, including Inverness-shire's own "Lake District" where there is a maze of tiny unclassified roads. (See section on North East Loch Ness for this area.)

The road from the forest car park dissects the forest, passing between the sheer sides of a steep ravine known as **The Pass of Inverfarigaig**, leading south eastwards to Errogie and Loch Mhor.

Near the Inverfarigaig end can be found a roadside **memorial to James Bryce**, a nineteenth century Irish geologist who fell and

James Bryce Memorial

died at this spot in 1877. The memorial was erected by "scientific friends in Edinburgh, Glasgow and Inverness."

The "Corkscrew"

Definitely not for the faint-hearted, a narrow, twisty, unclassified road climbs steeply from opposite the houses near the shore at Inverfarigaig to run to the east of the craggy outcrop Creag a Ghiubhais and high above the gorge of the River Farigaig. Loch Ness is largely shielded from sight by the crag but where the road stops climbing it is possible to take a short scramble onto the crest of the ridge

The "Corkscrew"

for superb views of the loch. There are spectacular views of the Monadhliath Mountains to the south east and ahead to Loch Ceol Glais and Loch Duntelchaig. This road eventually joins the B862 near Torness.

Scottish Highland Art

The stunning work of Ros Rowell

Near Torness is Edinuanagan Croft, the studio of Ros Rowell who paints beautiful, atmospheric watercolours of the Highlands, capturing the unique quality of the light on the hills in this part of the World in a highly distinctive way. This area is a wonderful place for artists and Ros runs a programme of workshops and classes for beginners through to experienced artists. She also sells original paintings, extremely reasonably priced original cards and limited edition prints. The studio and gallery are open for most of the year.

Loch Bran, high above Foyers on a minor road running between the B851 and the B852, is worth seeking out, especially in summer when it is covered in water lillies. A favoured breeding ground of several different species of dragonflies and damselflies, it is a designated Site of Special Scientific Interest.

Loch Mhor

Loch Mhor is a pretty loch which was once two separate waters. The observant may notice that the level of water appears to rise and fall regardless of the weather. This is because the loch feeds the hydro electric power station at Foyers, after which the water is pumped back up again. The small hamlet of **Errogie** and the pretty village of **Gorthleck** lie along

Hydro-electric scheme at Loch Mhor

Loch Mhor. Although less than twenty miles from Inverness, it is difficult to imagine that much has changed in this pocket of the Highlands over the last century.

It is claimed that **Bonnie Prince Charlie** had a narrow escape from the Redcoats by jumping out of an upstairs window at Gorthleck House, (Now called Gorthleck Mains.)

The **war memorial** between the two loch-side settlements enjoys a spectacular setting. Nearby, a causeway crosses the loch to the twin settlements of Wester and Easter Aberchalder, from where several tracks follow minor glens towards

War Memorial, Loch Mhor

some of the lesser peaks of the Monadhliath Mountains.

Loch Mhor Gallery is the home and studio of an extremely talented husband

Loch Mhor Gallery

and wife team. On display are stunning digital and traditional photographs, both colour and monochrome, of Highland

scenes as well as exquisite watercolour paintings on silk which have an almost ethereal quality.

The **River E** runs into Loch Mhor at Garthbeg. A minor road runs round the southern end of Loch Mhor before petering out into a track which follows the river for several miles into the mountains. For anyone who likes mature trees, there is a wonderful collection of beautiful **oak trees** along the minor road, half a mile from the B862. From **Garthbeg**, a path runs along the eastern side of Loch Mhor to the site of some **hut circles** on a piece of land jutting out into the loch. Near the start of the track are some lovely mature rowan trees.

Rowan trees on the shores of Loch Mhor

Public toilets
Fort Augustus main car park;
Opposite the entrance to the Falls of Foyers;
Farigaig Forest car park near Inverfarigaig.

23

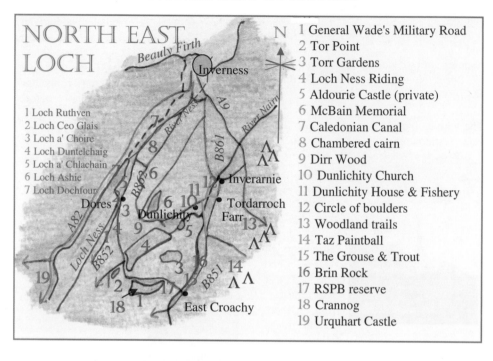

NORTH EAST LOCH

Beauly Firth
Inverness

1 Loch Ruthven
2 Loch Ceo Glais
3 Loch a' Choire
4 Loch Duntelchaig
5 Loch a' Chlachain
6 Loch Ashie
7 Loch Dochfour

Dores
Dunlichity
Inverarnie
Tordarroch
Farr
East Croachy

N

1 General Wade's Military Road
2 Tor Point
3 Torr Gardens
4 Loch Ness Riding
5 Aldourie Castle (private)
6 McBain Memorial
7 Caledonian Canal
8 Chambered cairn
9 Dirr Wood
10 Dunlichity Church
11 Dunlichity House & Fishery
12 Circle of boulders
13 Woodland trails
14 Taz Paintball
15 The Grouse & Trout
16 Brin Rock
17 RSPB reserve
18 Crannog
19 Urquhart Castle

Although most of the eastern side of Loch Ness lies in the shadow of the Monadhliath Range, the mountains drop away at the northern end. The River Nairn runs below the hills. Between the river and Loch Ness is an area of moorland and bogs, interspersed with a number of lochs and lochans sometimes called the "Inverness Lake District." It is an area of peace and beauty where a maze of unclassified roads wind their way unhurriedly from one tranquil loch view to another. Running parallel to Strathnairn but high above it, the River Findhorn cuts a steep path between the mountain peaks.

Other than Dores, there are a no sizeable villages in this area although there are several small settlements. It is a haven for bird watchers and wildlife spotters. To the north, Loch Ness becomes Loch Dochfour before splitting at Telford's weirs to become the River Ness and the Caledonian Canal.

The "Inverness Lake District"

North of Inverfarigaig, the B852 runs close to the shore, following the route of General Wade's Military Road. It is a single track road with passing places, running between birch and rowan trees and edged with many interesting plants and shrubs which make a colourful display amongst the prolific gorse and willowherb. Scenic at any time of the

The B852 north of Inverfarigaig

year, it is especially attractive in autumn. **Overhead ropeways** are intended to help the red squirrels cross the road safely. The pine forests here provide an ideal habitat for them, as amongst their favourite foods are pine seeds, larch cones and the fungi

Tor Point

which grow on the dark, damp ground between the trees. There are several loch

side **picnic areas**, the one opposite Urquhart Bay giving a view of Urquhart Castle from a less well known angle.

Dores

Dores, meaning "black wood," is a small village at the junction of the B852 and the B862 near **Tor Point**, which provides Loch Ness with its only beach.

Dores Beach

Near the small shingle beach there is parking, a small slipway and a quirky caravan selling refreshments and souvenirs. (Seasonal.)

Nessie?

From Dores it is possible to see for more than twenty miles down the length of the loch.

An excellent way to enjoy the view is

from the garden of **The Dores Inn,** which thoughtfully provides outdoor seating facing the loch. On cooler days, a cosy log fire burns indoors to welcome visitors. There is a good selection of home cooked food, as well as a large number of malt whiskies. Booking is recommended for the restaurant.

The Dores Inn

The village has a small post office but no other shops. The award winning **Pottery House B and B** is welcoming, comfortable and renowned for its freshly made breakfast rolls with homemade jams. There is free internet access for guests.

Across the road from the Dores Inn, a footpath leads up the hill to **Torr Gardens**. (Not to be confused with Tor Point.)

South of Dores, there are stunning views of Loch Ness from the B862 as it clings to the steep, heather-clad sides of The Great Glen.

A minor road dissects **Dirr Wood.** Here there are car parks and way-marked forest trails**.** Nearby, **Old Clune Wood** is also good for walking.

Also south of Dores, **Loch Ness Riding** provides hacking along 50 miles of tracks

South of Dores

through spectacular scenery. (Experienced riders only.)

At the side of an unclassified road a mile to the north east of Dores is a charming and quirky **woodland memorial** to members of the McBain clan. (Grid Ref: 613358) It was created in 1961 by Hughston McBain of McBain. Various metal plaques bear poems informing

The McBain Memorial

visitors that there are no remains buried here but exhorting people to be respectful anyway and not to steal the plants!

Strath Dores, immediately to the north of Dores, is an interesting area, reached via unclassified roads leading from the

B862, or on foot from Dores. A popular walk is from the beach, round wooded  **Tor Point** to **Aldourie Pier** and then past **Aldourie Castle** which is privately owned with no access to the castle grounds. In a fairy-tale setting, the castle was once a simple seventeenth century stone

Strath Dores

tower. Most of the present day structure was built in Victorian times. Beyond the castle the shore-side footpath joins a narrow road at Bona Ferry which leads to a beautiful oak woodland through which run several paths. The parish of Bona was the smallest in Inverness-shire until 1975, when it ceased to be a separate parish. A small ferry once operated across the water

The Bona Narrows

at this point, hence the name.
On the B862, just less than a mile south of Scaniport and next to the junction with a minor road, are the overgrown remains of a **chambered cairn.**

The Inverness "Lake District"

This area, to the south east of Dores, is bounded to the west by the B862 and to the east by the B851. Several minor roads wend their way between numerous lochs, making it difficult to adopt a single route without covering some ground twice so it is best approached as a series of loops. The area is a patchwork of rocky crags, peat bogs, beautiful isolated lochs and mixed woodland with many old trees. Consequently it is a haven for wildlife. The remains of a number of ancient settlements can be found in the form of cairns, hut circle sites, forts and **crannogs**. The latter are remnants of Celtic times when a family dwelling would be built on a small man-made island for defence purposes. It would be connected to the shore by a winding causeway just below the surface of the water so that outsiders would not know where it was.

From the B862 near Kindrummond a small road bears off north eastwards and then turns south to skirt the southern end of **Loch Ashie** and the northern shores of **Loch Duntelchaig**, the largest of the

Loch Duntelchaig

lochs in this area. Edged with rowan trees, this is a lovely, tranquil place to pause, also the start for several strolls or longer walks through the nearby forest. One signposted track runs for approximately three and half miles through the woods to **Bunachton** (Ordnance Survey map recommended.) Another particularly pleasant track follows the line of the eastern shore of Loch Duntelchaig before climbing towards isolated **Loch a Choire.**

Dunlichity

North east of Loch Duntelchaig, Dunlichity is a tiny hamlet with one of the most interesting churches and graveyards in Scotland. The first church here was

Dunlichity

founded by St. Finan in the seventh century, although the present church was built in 1758. Within and around the grounds are **enclosures** dedicated to different Clans and Clan chiefs, including the Shaws of Tordarroch, the MacGillivrays, the MacPhails and the Chiefs of The Clan

Unusual gravestones

Ay. Many gravestones have fascinating inscriptions and carvings, including one bearing testimony to a member of The Royal Company of Archers, The Queen's Bodyguard for Scotland. At the edge of the graveyard is a building which, after an internment,

Dunlichity Graveyard

would have served as a **watch tower** to guard against grave-robbers. Near the graveyard are the stones on which it is said the Jacobite followers of Bonnie Prince Charlie sharpened their swords, prior to the Battle of Culloden. **"The grave of the fifty"** is also reputed to be here – "the fifty" being cattle thieves from Lochaber who were surrounded and killed by locals then buried beyond the church grounds.

Dunlichity House, adjacent to the church, offers a high standard of guest house or self catering accommodation, alongside

Dunlichity House

its own **trout fishery** – a superb hidden retreat in spectacular countryside. Nearby are a **kiltmaker** and a **bee keeper**.

The Nairn Valley (Strathnairn.)

The River Nairn rises in the North West Monadhliath Mountains and occupies a

Strathnairn

wide, once-glaciated valley. Early settlers to its fertile plains left evidence of their presence in the form of **ring cairns**, various other arrangements of boulders and several sites where once stood **hut circles.**

Circle of boulders near Tordarroch

To the west of Tordarroch a large boulder circle can be seen between the road and the River Nairn.

Hares live in Strathnairn and can sometimes be seen.

At **Inverarnie** there are forest trails in **Littlemill Wood**, a Site of Special Scientific Interest. These go to ridges and kettle hole lochans created during the Ice Age. In the village is **Inverarnie Stores**, an excellent licensed grocer selling such diverse wares as eggs, logs, calor gas, daily papers, bedding plants and second hand books.

There are several community woodlands in Strathnairn. **School Wood** near **Farr** is an interesting place to explore with way-marked paths, information boards, picnic tables and a shelter to enjoy the outdoors in less than clement weather. Nearby

School Wood, Farr

Milton Wood is another community forest with trails and picnic areas.

Milton Wood

Off the B851 between Farr and Croachy is **Taz Paintball** set in a large area of woodland. (Signposted "Garbole 8 miles.")

Brin Rock is a dramatic crag which rises to 435 metres. In its shadow is **Brin Herb Nursery**, normally open from April to September. Incorporating a tea room and a shop selling Scottish foodstuffs, this is a

RSPB reserve, Loch Ruthven

Brin Rock & Brin Herb Nursery

good place to stock up on picnic goodies! **Internet access** is also available here.

On the B851, just north of East Croachy, is **The Steadings at The Grouse and Trout.** The hotel and restaurant was once the original Flitchity Inn. In beautiful surroundings, there are panoramic views over the surrounding countryside. This has long been MacGillivray country and a life sized stag sculpture stands proudly at the gates to commemorate the long association of the clan with this part of Strathnairn.

Loch Ruthven.
Loch Ruthven lies between the B851 and the B862. The loch and the area of birch woodland, moors and crags around it, form an **RSPB bird reserve**. At the

eastern end is a car park. The loch is unique for its population of rare red and gold Slavonian Grebe, this being their only Scottish breeding ground. There are also rare red throated divers and many other species of bird including sandpipers and willow warblers. At the western end of Loch Ruthven is a small artificial island known as a **crannog.** (See page 27 for definition.) Nearby, on the shore, is a further fortification from the same period.

Ancient earthworks, Loch Ruthven

Internet Access
Brin Herb Nursery

SOUTH WEST LOCH NESS

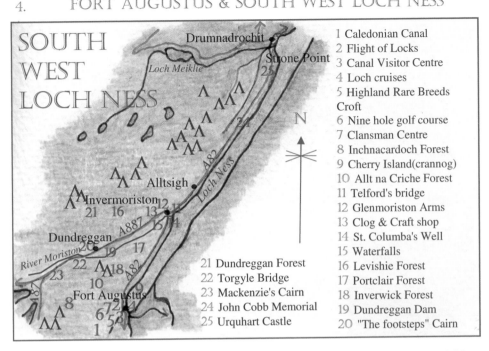

1 Caledonian Canal
2 Flight of Locks
3 Canal Visitor Centre
4 Loch cruises
5 Highland Rare Breeds Croft
6 Nine hole golf course
7 Clansman Centre
8 Inchnacardoch Forest
9 Cherry Island(crannog)
10 Allt na Criche Forest
11 Telford's bridge
12 Glenmoriston Arms
13 Clog & Craft shop
14 St. Columba's Well
15 Waterfalls
16 Levishie Forest
17 Portclair Forest
18 Inverwick Forest
19 Dundreggan Dam
20 "The footsteps" Cairn
21 Dundreggan Forest
22 Torgyle Bridge
23 Mackenzie's Cairn
24 John Cobb Memorial
25 Urquhart Castle

Loch Lochy and Loch Oich sit along the Great Glen but only at the sight of Loch Ness can one can grasp the scale of the massive fault line which runs from one side of Scotland to the other. To the west are Glen Garry and Glen Moriston but north eastwards the mighty loch stretches for twenty-three miles from Fort Augustus almost to Inverness, the steep sides of the valley hinting at the great depth of the water and giving the loch a brooding majesty. The western side of the loch is by far the busier of the two, the A82 running next to the loch for almost its entire length with several large lay-bys providing good vantage points. The land rises steeply from the shore, up through forest to dramatic craggy peaks. The Great Glen Way runs above and parallel to the A82. Half way along the loch, at Strone Point, and dominating the view from either direction are the ruins of Urquhart Castle, one of Scotland's most imposing and well known castles.

Fort Augustus

Once named Kilchuimeim, after St. Chuimeim who established a church here, Fort Augustus gained its present name after the 1715 Jacobite uprising. The fort here was named after King George's younger son, Prince William Augustus (later Duke of Cumberland.) In 1730

Fort Augustus

31

General Wade enlarged the fort but in 1745 it was captured and largely destroyed by Bonnie Prince Charlie's supporters before being rebuilt by The Duke of Cumberland. Later it became the site of a Benedictine Abbey, established in 1876 and in use until 1998. The Abbey buildings, now redeveloped, are impressive.

Fort Augustus is a lively, bustling village and the main gateway to Loch Ness from the south: The A82, The Great Glen Way for both walkers and cyclists and The Caledonian Canal all converge here, the latter

Nesssie !

providing a major tourist attraction where the canal descends twelve metres through a dramatic flight of locks right in the centre of the village. This is also a good place for spotting the Loch Ness Monster, or at least a large canal-side model of it! A swing bridge allows boats through to

Fort Augustus Swing Bridge

the final short stretch of canal before it enters Loch Ness, accompanied by the rivers Oich and Tarff which also join the loch here, to either side of the canal.

Fort Augustus has a wide range of facilities including numerous hotels and guest houses, a filling station, garage, post office, tourist information, supermarket and off licence and several nice souvenir shops. There is an abundance of good restaurants and cafes, too many to mention them all. The **Scottish Kitchen,** opposite the main car park, offers an excellent all-day choice but of particular note is the breakfast menu. At night the cafe becomes a restaurant with imaginative nightly specials. Also worthy of mention is the canal-side **Chip Shop** with a mind boggling number of things to eat with chips!

The nearby **Lock Inn** is popular for both bar meals and a full restaurant menu. (Also a wonderful collection of malt whiskies, complete with log fire beside which to enjoy them.) For an iconic view from the shore, try the

A warm welcome....

Boathouse Restaurant. Alternatively, **The Lovat Loch Ness** on the main street is the place to be pampered with log fires, spa treatments and top cuisine in one of two restaurants. For self caterers there is a first rate **butcher's shop** on the canal side selling homemade bridies, haggis and black pudding as well as freshly baked Scotch pies. **West End Garage** offers an efficient 24 hour vehicle recovery service. There is a **nine hole golf course** where clubs and trolleys may be hired. **The Caledonian Canal Visitor Centre.** The canal visitor centre, in a converted

Caledonian Canal Visitor Centre

lockkeeper's cottage, has fascinating displays about the building of the canal and its ongoing maintenance.

Stanley level from Telford's era

A Stanley level from Telford's era is one exhibit. There is a tempting selection of stylish gifts and a good selection of books. Admission is free.

Just off the main road, at the bottom of the locks, is a small, attractive **memorial garden** commemorating Queen Victoria's Jubilee. The **Iceberg Glassblowing Studio** can be found on the main road.

Memorial for Queen Victoria's Jubilee

Loch Ness Cruises
Several companies offer cruises on the canal and the loch, the latter ranging from

Loch Ness Cruises

traditional pleasure cruisers to speed boat trips. Some vessels boast on-board sonar displays for monster spotting! **The Highland Rare Breeds Croft** is a delightful 20 acre park next to the River Oich and signposted from the main road along a lovely riverside walk. Highland

The Highland Rare Breeds Croft

33

cattle, red deer, unusual sheep, goats, ducks, geese and rabbits offer a warm welcome to children and grown-ups alike. The **Clansman Centre**, next to the swing bridge, is a former lock-keeper's cottage which now houses an interesting museum with live shows about Highland life and a gift shop specialising in Celtic designs. **Mountain Bikes** may be hired from Caledonian House B and B on the lock side.

The Great Glen Trading Centre at the filling station sells a wide range of foodstuffs as well as clothing and an extensive selection of Scottish giftware. On the main street **Glen Albyn Gifts** sells very reasonably priced gifts and souvenirs. A modern telephone box on the main street has **emailing and texting** facilities, whilst there is a **Wi Fi hotspot** for laptops at the top of the locks.

Walks around Fort Augustus

Riverside walk, Fort Augustus

There are a number of interesting walks in and around Fort Augustus. A pleasant, gentle stroll between the canal and the River Oich follows the tow path south to **Kytra Lock**, just over two miles from Fort Augustus. In the other direction, a path runs alongside the short stretch of canal from the swing bridge to where the canal enters Loch Ness. West of Fort Augustus is **Inchnacardoch Forest** which has many way-marked paths.

Fort Augustus to Invermoriston

Just North of Fort Augustus is **Cherry Island**, the three thousand year old remains of a man-made island called a crannog, upon which there would once have been a dwelling. (This, incidentally, is the only remaining island in Loch Ness.) Beyond Fort Augustus, the A82 follows the shore of the loch through mixed woodland. **Allt na Criche Forest** was the first land purchased by the Forestry Commission. Some of the conifers here were planted by Lord Lovat who founded the organisation. There are numerous **forest tracks** here for walking and mountain biking.

Invermoriston, six miles north of Fort Augustus and just over twenty seven miles south of Inverness, is an attractive village. "Inver" means "mouth of" and

Invermoriston

this is where the River Moriston tumbles down waterfalls and rushes under a beautiful **old stone double-arched bridge** before joining Loch Ness. The bridge was built by Telford and was in

use until 1933.
The best view of it can be obtained from the small road signposted "Dalcataig." A plaque nearby details its history, including the fact that the bridge took far longer to build than anticipated due to "a languid and inattentive contractor!"

Telford's bridge, Invermoriston

Salmon can sometimes be seen leaping up the waterfall. Near the bridge is **The Old Smithy**, now an outdoor activity centre with accommodation but operating as a blacksmith's until 1966. The village was once the site of a sawmill, the wood being transported by boat along the loch. Steam boats used to call at Glen Moriston. The attractive **Glenmoriston Arms Hotel** dates from 1740 and was originally a drovers' inn. Parts of the old inn remain - the Moriston Bar has granite walls which are three feet thick. Open fires, an extensive wine list and over one hundred and fifty single malt whiskies make this a welcoming place. Famous previous guests have included Boswell and Johnson, Gavin Maxwell, Charlie Chaplin and Princess Margaret.
At the junction is the excellent **Glen Moriston Stores and post office** with something for everyone: On sale are wines and spirits, groceries, bread &

milk, newspapers, souvenirs, fishing rod hire, guide books, fruit & vegetables, tea and coffee, hot pies and blister plasters (!) Round the corner, on the Skye road, is

Glenmoriston Stores

the **Glen Rowan Cafe** and the unique **Clog and Craft Shop** selling high quality clogs and leather bush hats, all hand-crafted on the premises.

Hand crafted clogs

The Great Glen Way passes through Invermoriston and there are also several shorter paths along the river, down to the loch and in the forest. **Way-marked paths** lead from the main car park where there are information boards. Downstream from the bridge is a **summer house** from where there are the best views of the river and the main waterfall. During the season, salmon leap up the waterfall on their annual journey upstream. Behind the main car park can often be found some friendly highland cattle who are usually glad to pose for photographs. From near the Clog and Craft shop a way-marked track leads upwards for panoramic views of the loch. **St. Columba's Well,** or Fuaran-Choluim-Chille to give it its Gaelic name, is down some steps near the shop. This natural spring is thought to have been blessed by

St. Columba's Well

St. Columba when he passed this way in the sixth century on his way to visit Brude, the Pictish King. (Prior to this the waters from the well were thought to be cursed.) A plaque tells the story. **Glenmoriston House** (privately owned) is the fourth house to be built on this site. The first and second were burned down as reprisals for Glenmoriston's support of the Jacobite cause. The third was accidentally destroyed by fire.

Email and texting is available at the telephone box by the main car park.

The village is also a major junction, the A887 branching off to the West through **Glen Moriston** to Glen Shiel and beyond to Lochalsh and The Isle of Skye. Travelling south an alternative route is to detour through Glen Moriston as far as Bun Loyne and then take the A87 through Glen Garry.

(For Glen Garry see page 11.)

Glen Moriston

Glen Moriston stretches west to Loch Cluanie, out of which the River Moriston

River Moriston

flows to be joined by the Rivers Loyne and Doe on its route to Loch Ness. The lower reaches of the glen are cool and shady where the river flows between the heavily wooded lower reaches of Levishie Forest to the north and the Portclair and Inverwick Forests to the south.

Roadside oak trees

Four miles west of Invermoriston is **Dundreggan Resevoir.** Many feet beneath the dam is a hydro-electric power station, the water passing down a shaft to turn turbines to generate electricity before travelling along a tunnel twenty feet in diameter and nearly four miles long into Loch Ness. The dam contains a special fish pass so that salmon may continue their journey along the river.

Dundreggan

Dundreggan means "hill of the dragon." It is one of those places which people tend to rush past and miss things of interest. **The Redburn Cafe** is open Tuesday to Sunday for excellent snacks and meals, information and gifts. (Be warned: The giant bacon baguette here is too good to share!) **"The footsteps"** - just west of the cafe is a roadside **cairn** marking the place where, in 1827, a travelling preacher who had been heckled declared that his footprints would remain there for ever more to prove that he was speaking the truth. Legend has it that the grass will not grow there and his footprints may still be seen.

From the cairn an old drovers' road, known as **Eve's Road**, climbs high into **Dundreggan Forest** to descend on the other side at Tomich near the entrance to Glen Affric.

To the south west, high on a ridge in Beinneun Forest, can be seen the wind turbines of **The Millennium Wind Farm** standing out against the sky. West of Dundreggan, **Torgyle Bridge** is another of Telford's creations. Two miles beyond is signposted an **old military road,** now a track which runs for about eight miles through **Inchnacardoch Forest** to Fort Augustus.

Further west, two miles before the A887 is joined by the A87, is **M a c k e n z i e ' s Cairn.** After the B a t t l e o f Culloden, seven men from Glen M o r i s t o n sheltered the

Mackenzie's Cairn

defeated Bonnie Prince Charlie in local caves. Roderick Mackenzie, a brave loyalist lookalike "of the same size and of similar resemblance to His Royal Prince" was captured and killed, providing valuable time for the real prince to make his escape. The roadside memorial stands at the place where Mackenzie fell. Nearby is the entrance to the **Ceannacroc Power Station**. Locked gates prevent access by vehicles but pedestrians can use the track which follows the path of the **River Doe** high into the hills, past waterfalls and a dam. This is a seriously scenic walk, the track makes for easy going but it is all uphill.

To complete the Glen Moriston/Glen Garry loop, take the A87 south to the A82 at Invergarry. (see section on South of Loch Ness for details about Glen Garry.)

Invermoriston to Urquhart Castle.

North of Invermoriston, the A82 closely follows Loch Ness with panoramic views from several roadside lay-bys. (Great care must be taken when crossing the A82.) In spring primroses, bluebells and ferns cling to the steep rocks at the side of the road. In summer these give way to brilliant yellow gorse and the area is renowned for the huge numbers of butterflies to be seen. At Alltsigh is a **youth hostel**.

There are good views across the loch to the hydro electric works at Foyers.

About two miles south of Urquhart Castle stands a **Memorial to John Cobb**, once holder of the World Land Speed Record. He was killed near here in 1952 whilst setting a new World Water Speed Record in his boat "Crusader." He achieved two hundred and six miles an hour before disaster struck: As the boat slowed down

John Cobb Memorial

it began to bounce on the water and fell apart. The remains of the boat are still on

Plaque to John Cobb

the bottom of the loch. In a lay-by on the opposite side of the road are a series of interesting information boards about his achievements, with some reproductions of contemporary photographs.

Urquhart Castle. The ruins of Urquhart Castle sit strategically on Strone Point at the entrance to Urquhart Bay near where the Rivers Enrick and Coiltie enter Loch Ness. Protruding almost into the loch itself, it is very imposing and is one of Scotland's iconic castles.
There is a large car park overlooking the castle. The main entrance to the ruins is via an excellent visitor centre with a good audio visual presentation. The castle's

precise origins are uncertain but there has certainly been a fortification at this point since Pictish times and a substantial castle probably since at least the thirteenth century, with additions made over subsequent centuries. The castle has been much fought over, ownership changing hands frequently over the

Urquhart Castle

centuries. It was finally reduced to a ruin in the seventeenth century by government forces who blew it up with gunpowder to avoid the Jacobites establishing a stronghold here. However, there is sufficient left of the original to provide a fascinating insight into the castle's past. Present day facilities include a large gift shop, cafe and audio visual displays.

Public Toilets
Fort Augustus, in the main car park near the filling station
Invermoriston Memorial Hall in the main car park
Drumnadrochit car park
Internet
Modern telephone boxes at Fort Augustus (main street) and Invermoriston (car park)
Wi fi hot spot – top of the locks at Fort Augustus.

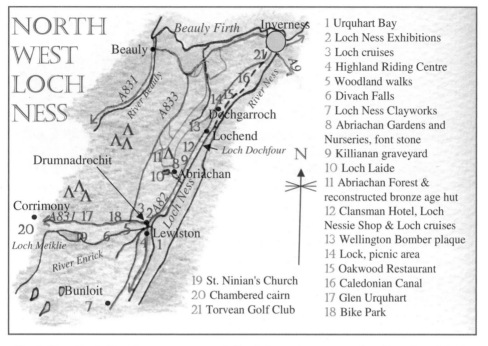

NORTH WEST LOCH NESS

1 Urquhart Bay
2 Loch Ness Exhibitions
3 Loch cruises
4 Highland Riding Centre
5 Woodland walks
6 Divach Falls
7 Loch Ness Clayworks
8 Abriachan Gardens and Nurseries, font stone
9 Killianan graveyard
10 Loch Laide
11 Abriachan Forest & reconstructed bronze age hut
12 Clansman Hotel, Loch Nessie Shop & Loch cruises
13 Wellington Bomber plaque
14 Lock, picnic area
15 Oakwood Restaurant
16 Caledonian Canal
17 Glen Urquhart
18 Bike Park
19 St. Ninian's Church
20 Chambered cairn
21 Torvean Golf Club

North West Loch Ness is more commercialised than other parts and well equipped for its many visitors - especially those seeking the Loch Ness Monster! Drumnadrochit, situated roughly half way along Loch Ness at the head of Urquhart Bay, is a bustling tourist centre with all the amenities one would expect to find in such a place. North of Drumnadrochit, the A82 clings to the loch shore until reaching the small settlement of Lochend, where the loch does indeed end. Along this stretch of the main road there are a number of lay-bys from which the loch can be admired. It is an extremely popular route and great care should be taken when crossing the A82. It is a very busy road and drivers' attention is easily diverted from the road towards the water.

North West Loch Ness is an area of great contrast: To the west of the main road, Glen Urquhart, Abriachan Forest and Loch Laide are beautiful areas often overlooked in favour of the more obvious attractions of the Loch. There are beautiful glens, secluded lochs and steep ravines where dramatic waterfalls plunge between sheer walls of rock.

All things Nessie !

39

Drumnadrochit

Drumnadrochit has a wide range of facilities for visitors, including Loch Ness Monster exhibitions, restaurants, accommodation, boat trips, a pharmacy, bank, gift shops and other retail outlets. Garage facilities are available at neighbouring **Lewiston**.

The most frequently asked question at the post office concerns pedestrian access to **Loch Ness.** The answer is not immediately obvious, being down Kilmore Road and along a woodland walk, crossing a river into another small wood and all preferably wearing wellies! There is a large car park in the centre of the village where the **Tourist Information Centre** and **public toilets** can be found. The main street is lined with various shops and cafes. In the middle of the village is a pretty green featuring an impressive **model of Urquhart Castle.**

"The Original Loch Ness MonsterExhibition"

Floral model of Urquhart Castle

There are two different Loch Ness exhibitions in the village:

The Original Loch Ness Monster Exhibition

This intriguing and fun exhibition embraces all the mystery and romance surrounding the Loch Ness Monster and concentrates on the numerous sightings there have been over the years, including the many fakes and hoaxes. Visitors are left to make up their own minds! A wide screen cinema brings the subject vividly to life with simultaneous translations into several different languages. Adjoining the centre is a large shop selling a huge range of Scottish gifts, whiskies, foodstuffs, clothing, jewellery and much more. A **model railway** with miniature steam engines adds to the fun. Cruises on the loch can be booked here - the vessel "Nessie Hunter" has sonar and underwater cameras.

The Loch Ness 2000 Exhibition Centre

This exhibition details the vast amount of research carried out around Loch Ness over the years and the many projects which have tried to establish the truth about the so-called Loch Ness Monster. Themed sections explore the mystery of the loch in a thought provoking way, including underwater photographs and a multimedia presentation. Loch Ness cruises are available aboard the vessel "Deepscan," named after the 1987 project to scan the loch. The on-board sonar equipment offers a fascinating alternative view of the loch.

There are also several retail outlets including a **kilt maker**, an **ancestral research centre, a specialist whisky**

Loch Ness 2000

shop and shops selling clothing and souvenirs, as well as **woodland walks**, a **water garden, cafe, bar/restaurant** and **picnic area.**

Specialist whisky shop

The Clansman Gift Company opposite the main car park is a fascinating shop selling a wide range of Scottish and Loch Ness themed gifts and souvenirs. **Boat trips** on the loch can be booked here.

The **post office,** which is also an off licence and general store, is particularly well stocked. Look no further for

groceries, birthday cards, dog food, books, calor gas, fishing flies, post cards, souvenirs and fresh cream cakes!

Fiddlers Bar has won awards for its selection of single malt whiskies and limited edition ales, including Great Glen Way Ale.

At the junction of the A82 and A831 is a **war memorial** with an interesting castle sculpted on top of the cross.

Fiddlers Bar

The Highland Riding Centre at Borlum Farm, Lewiston, is a major centre for **Riding For The Disabled** but treks and tuition are also available daily to able bodied visitors.

Craigmonie and Balmacaan Woodland Walks

Balmacaan Wood is owned by the Woodland Trust for Scotland. Since 1984 there has been much restoration of natural woodland. Craigmonie is owned by the Forestry Commission. The two organizations have worked in partnership to develop a network of way-marked paths through the two woods. Roe deer, red squirrel and pine marten can sometimes be spotted in the woods. More elusive are the badgers which also make their home here. An excellent leaflet/map which is available from the Visit Scotland Centre details several routes, as well as an interesting history of the Balmacaan estate.

The Divach Falls

From the southern part of the village a minor road leads past the Loch Ness Inn and a row of cottages, several of which are B and B's. There are several **woodland walks** signposted before the road begins to climb to the Divach Falls, high above Drumnadrochit. From the steeply winding road there are fabulous views over the loch. At the top is a small car park from which a gateway opens on to a pretty path which makes its way between oak trees to the falls - a spectacular sight as the Divach Burn plunges over 100 feet (30m.) A painting of the Divach Falls by artist John Phillips hangs in Buckingham Palace.

High above Drumnadrochit

The Bunloit Road

Signposted from Lewiston is Bunloit and the **Loch Ness Clayworks**. This dead end road is particularly pretty. Situated at the end is the pottery which produces a wide range of ceramics both useful and attractive. There is also a small hill walkers' car park, the starting point for the ascent to **Meall Fuar-mhonaidh**, a popular walk. Along this road, for anyone needing to find good quality care for canine members of the family, is

Drumnadrochit Boarding Kennels (recommended by Molly Labrador and Megan Cairn Terrier who have been known to occasionally take a short break there.)

There are several hotels and inns in the village. At the southern end of the village, is **The Loch Ness Inn,** (formerly the Lewiston Arms Hotel) offering a friendly welcome to everyone. Situated on the Great Glen Way, this is a popular stopping off point for walkers. It has a special walkers' bar, beer garden, large restaurant with wood burning stove and an all day menu. At the other end of the village is the comfortable, family owned **Drumnadrochit Hotel** with bar, restaurant and upstairs viewing lounge.

The privately owned and atmospheric **Loch Ness Lodge Hotel** dates from 1740

The Loch Ness Lodge Hotel

and is set amidst woodland. It has an all day coffee shop and restaurant.
The Benleva Hotel offers accommodation and cask ale in a fully renovated three hundred year old manse. The original village "hanging" tree still stands in the garden! A footpath runs from the hotel to the shores of the loch.

Glen Urquhart

Glen Urquhart

From the junction in the centre of Drumnadrochit, the A831 runs west into Glen Urquhart or Glen Urchadainn to give it its Gaelic name. (Meaning "wooded glen.") It is the route of the River Enrick which runs into and out of Loch Meiklie. As both sides of the glen are forested for much of its length, it is an excellent place for spotting deer and other wildlife.

Rising beyond Drumnadrochit is **Craigmony Hill**, named after the eleventh century Nordic Prince Monie who hid there after a battle before being killed as he tried to escape down the glen. Along the glen are several B and B's as well as self catering accommodation. In **Glen Urquhart Forest** there are picnic

Balnain Bike Park

sites and **way marked trails. Balnain Bike Park** is a dedicated forest mountain biking park.

The Steadings Country Pub is a welcoming, no-frills family pub. There is a large function room which is available for groups. Open from 5pm till late, Monday to Saturday and from 1pm Sundays, for a wide choice of reasonably priced food.

Bearnock Country Centre offers

Bearnock Country Centre

accommodation in an idyllic setting amongst birch woods. There are five cottages, two log cabins and an independent five star hostel which is open all year round, immaculately clean and which has en suite facilities to every room. Kitchen facilities are excellent and there is also a small shop.

St Ninian's Church is an extremely pretty, white Scottish Episcopal church five miles west of Drumnadrochit on the shores of Loch Meiklie. St. Ninian was a fifth century saint who travelled widely, converting the Picts to

St. Ninian's Church

Christianity. After St. Ninian's time many of the Picts went back to Paganism until the arrival of St. Columba a century later. A lovely gnarled old oak tree stands in the church grounds.

The Glen Urquhart House Hotel, overlooking Loch Meiklie, is a comfortable hotel set in six acres of grounds and serving Scottish food in its "Ghillies Lair" restaurant. Alternative accommodation is available in wooden lodges set within the hotel grounds.

Abriachan Gardens & Nurseries

At **Corrimony** is the site of a fairly well preserved **chambered cairn**, guarded by a circle of **standing stones.** In the passage leading into the chamber are some mysterious **cup and ring marks.** Nearby is an **RSPB reserve,** amongst stunning moorland and forest. Beyond, to the west, is **Cannich**, gateway to Strathglass and beautiful Glen Affric.

Abriachan

Mid way between Inverness and Drumnadrochit, Abriachan is not so much a village as an area. A constant stream of motorists rush by on the A82, not realising what they are missing. There is a small car park on the opposite side of the road to the loch. From here **waymarked trails** lead off into the forest, as well as this being used as a car park for Abriachan Gardens. On the other side of the road, a track leads down to the remains of **Abriachan Pier,** no longer in use but once of vital importance as a landing stage for the steam ferries which transported people and goods before the present road was built.

Abriachan Gardens & Nurseries

"Just another garden" this is **not**! This is three acres of pure magic, the culmination of over twenty five years' work. Set in stunning hillside scenery between loch and mountain, the garden contains rare and unusual plants from all over the world as well as some old fashioned plant varieties. There are twisting pathways, secret arbours, surprise sculptures and breathtaking views of the loch (with plenty of sitting places from which to enjoy them.) The garden is crowned by a ring of majestic oaks and, if all this were not enough, hidden in the gardens is a mysterious "**font stone.**" There are several legends about its origin but it possibly dates from the time of St.

The Font Stone

Garden suprises!

Columba's visit to King Brude. The hollow in the stone is said to always contain water no matter how dry the weather.

Allow time for an unhurried visit – the owners are even happy for you to bring your own picnic. (Free admission to RHS members.) In addition to the small car park just off the road, there is space for disabled parking within the grounds.

Killianan Churchyard, just below the gardens, is an ancient graveyard with some interesting gravestones. There was probably once a chapel on the site but no trace of one remains. A special stone is said to have been used to pledge one year trial marriages.

Ancient gravestones

Loch Laide
Signposted "Abriachan," a steep road runs from the A82 to high above Loch Ness. (If approaching from the south, it is necessary to use the turning place on the right hand side of the A82 to access this

Loch Laide

Abriachan Forest

smaller road.) There are stunning views of Loch Ness far below. A left fork near the top of the hill leads to Loch Laide. A small roadside lay-by is the perfect place to enjoy spectacular reflections in this tranquil loch, especially in autumn.

Abriachan Forest Trust
Beyond Loch Laide is the greater part of Abriachan Forest containing native woodland of birch, hazel and oak. Since 1998 the woods have been owned by the community. An imaginative development has been the creation of a "**forest school**" for outdoor learning. Facilities for both

Reconstructed Bronze Age hut

locals and visitors include **forest trails** for walking and **mountain biking** and extensive informative displays about the varied terrain. In addition to forest there are heather moorlands and areas of peat bog. The whole forest is a dynamic wonderland with something exciting to discover at every turn: There are **tree houses**, **adventure playgrounds**, a **dragonfly pond**, **hides** for watching wildlife, **picnic and barbeque facilities**, a reconstructed **Bronze Age hut** and reconstructed **sheilings** to explore. (Sheilings were the simple shelters which were used in summer by those people tending the livestock which had been herded on to higher ground to graze.)

The Clansman Hotel & Cobbs Restaurant, on the A82 north of Drumnadrochit, overlook the loch and enjoy stunning views, the hotel having a spacious observation lounge. This is an excellent place for an overnight

The Clansman Hotel

Nessie Souvenirs

stop in conjunction with a cruise on the loch from the **Clansman Harbour**. Adjacent to the hotel the **Loch Ness Nessie**

Shop offers an enormous choice of reasonably priced Scottish and local gifts and souvenirs, a tempting range of single malt whiskies, a coffee shop overlooking

A tempting choice!

the loch and hourly boat trips from the on-site harbour. Nearby, stands one of the few remaining old fashioned AA boxes.

Wellington Bomber Memorial

Two miles south of Lochend, alongside the narrow part of the loch, is a long lay-by at which there is a memorial and information boards descibing the raising of a

Wellington Bomber memorial

Wellington Bomber which crashed into the loch in 1940 and lay undiscovered until 1976. The Wellington was on a training flight but suffered catastrophic engine failure. Most of the crew bailed out while the captain and co pilot managed to land the plane on the loch and escape before it sank. The only fatality was one crew member whose parachute failed to open. In 1984 the aircraft was raised from the loch bed and is now restored and on display at Brooklands Museum in Surrey. A nearby plaque shows a copy of the sonar chart of the loch with the plane clearly visible beneath the water.

Public Toilets
Main car park Drumnadrochit
Loch Ness Clansman Hotel & Gifts
Abriachan forest

---

6. NORTH OF LOCH NESS, LOCHEND TO INVERNESS

For this section please see map of NW Loch Ness on page 39.

The northern end of Loch Ness squeezes into the Bona Narrows, where Loch Ness becomes Loch Dochfour, a man-made loch which was created when Telford built a weir to raise the level of Loch Ness by nine feet during the construction of the Caledonian Canal. It is near this point where Saint Columba is reputed to have seen his mythical waterbeast. The saint was on his way to meet with the Pictish King Brude whose seat was high in the hills a few miles north of this point.

The Caledonian Canal north of Loch Ness

Beyond the weir the River Ness and The Caledonian Canal run side by side for just over three of the river's total six mile length, the two stretches of water being separated only by a narrow strip of land along which the canal towpath runs. This length of the canal/River Ness is a bustling place with plenty of activity from passing boats as they negotiate the locks. The tow path is a pleasant place to walk and can be followed right into the heart of the Inverness.

Loch Dochfour
For a short way the A82 runs along a narrow causeway through the edge of Loch Dochfour. On one side of the road is picturesque Dochfour House, which has been owned by the Baillie family since the fifteenth century. The present Georgian house replaced the original which was burned down during the 1745 Jacobite uprising. The eastern side of Loch Dochfour is forested with mixed woodland (including some lovely old oak trees,) criss-crossed with paths and tracks accessible from the B862 Inverness/Dores road. From this side of the loch are views of an interesting Octagonal house which from 1919 housed the original navigation light for vessels entering or leaving the Narrows.

The original Bonar "lighthouse"

Dochgarroch
Dochgarroch is a popular place with lots to see. There are always boats moored here on their way between Loch Ness and Inverness. There are **way-marked walks**, **picnic tables** and access to the other side of the canal via the locks. **Dochgarroch Locks,** built by Telford,

Dochgarroch Lock

are unusually wide because they were originally intended to accommodate the passage of large ships, although by the time the canal was completed rail transport would soon take over from the canals. A minor **earthquake** in 1901, centred on Dochgarroch, left a crack half an inch wide along a six hundred metre stretch of the towpath.

The Oakwood Restaurant and Gift Shop offers an exciting and imaginative menu all year round, although with reduced hours in winter. (Lamb roasted with lemon and garlic is definitely a house speciality!) Gluten free and vegan diets catered for with prior notice. Tel: 01463 861481. Take your own wine.

Further along the A82 towards Inverness, the **Dunain Park Hotel** offers a high standard of accommodation and food in lovely surroundings.

Torvean Golf Course, on the south west outskirts of the city of Inverness, is an eighteen hole course next to the Caledonian Canal. Torvean was once the site of a battle between the MacDonald Lord of the Isles and Duncan Mackintosh, the Governor's son. Torvean means MacBean's Hill.

A swing bridge carries the A82 over the Caledonian Canal into the City of Inverness. By the swing bridge is the home of Jacobite Cruises.

Jacobite Experience Loch Ness

Canal & Loch Ness cruises

This company offer a wide range of tour options for cruising Loch Ness or the Caledonian Canal, by coach from Inverness or from the Clansman Harbour

The Jacobite Queen

between Inverness and Drumnadrochit. Some options include a tour of Urquhart Castle. Tel: 01463 233999 website: www.jacobite.co.uk

CITY OF INVERNESS

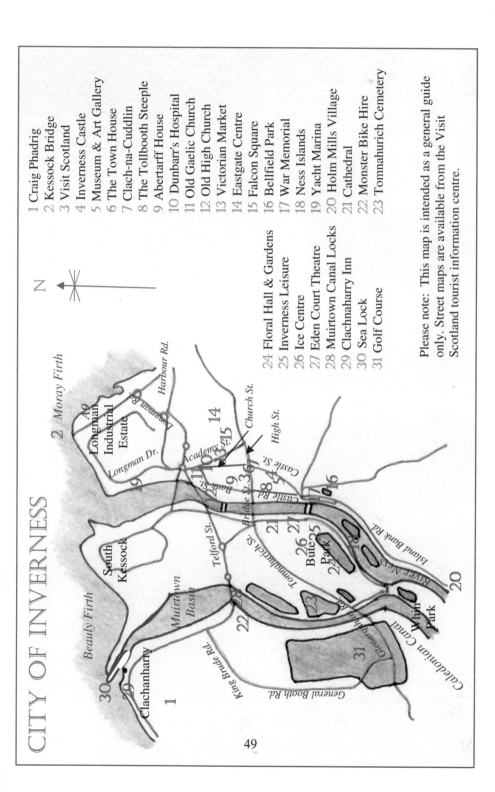

1 Craig Phadrig
2 Kessock Bridge
3 Visit Scotland
4 Inverness Castle
5 Museum & Art Gallery
6 The Town House
7 Clach-na-Cuddin
8 The Tollbooth Steeple
9 Abertarff House
10 Dunbar's Hospital
11 Old Gaelic Church
12 Old High Church
13 Victorian Market
14 Eastgate Centre
15 Falcon Square
16 Bellfield Park
17 War Memorial
18 Ness Islands
19 Yacht Marina
20 Holm Mills Village
21 Cathedral
22 Monster Bike Hire
23 Tommahurich Cemetery

24 Floral Hall & Gardens
25 Inverness Leisure
26 Ice Centre
27 Eden Court Theatre
28 Muirtown Canal Locks
29 Clachnaharry Inn
30 Sea Lock
31 Golf Course

Please note: This map is intended as a general guide only. Street maps are available from the Visit Scotland tourist information centre.

INVERNESS

Inverness is an attractive and vibrant place, straddling the River Ness. Its Gaelic name, "Inbhir Nis," translates as "mouth of the Ness." Although long considered the capital of the Highlands and created a Royal Burgh in 1158 by King David, Inverness was only officially granted the status of "City" in the year 2000 for the Millennium - even though

there has been a settlement here since prehistoric times and it was the capital of the ancient Pictish Kingdom. King Brude is thought to have had his fort on top of Craig Phadrig to the west of Inverness. When St. Columba arrived there in AD565 he was refused admittance. Legend has it that, undaunted, the saint made the sign of the cross and caused the massive doors of the fort to open by themselves. The Pictish king was so awed by this apparent act of God that he was immediately converted to Christianity.

Welcome to Inverness

As Inverness grew the town prospered as a fishing port with a thriving ship building industry and an export trade in wool, furs, wood and other goods. However, being strategically the gateway to the north of Scotland, where routes from all directions converge, control of Inverness has been much fought over through the ages. Consequently, it has a lively history involving not a small amount of bloodshed and which has caused extensive unsettled periods right up until the nineteenth century when the troublesome Highlanders were finally brought under the control of the English government. As the political climate became more settled, Inverness gained importance as a centre of trade. It was one of the main centres on the droving routes for cattle being taken south, had a well established wool market and did a brisk trade in hardy ponies for the pits of Northumberland and Durham.

The town continued to develop during the eighteenth century but it was during the nineteenth century, with the building of the Caledonian Canal and the arrival of the railway, that Inverness began to take on its modern appearance. Queen Victoria's love of Scotland and her trips through the Caledonian Canal to Inverness furthered its popularity as a fashionable holiday destination, becoming known as "The Royal Route."

Many new municipal buildings were erected and additional bridges were built across the Ness. Industry continued to develop with ship building, distilling, fishing and, later, engineering all providing employment which in turn drew people towards the town and furthered its growth.

City by the river

Today, Inverness is the major administrative centre for the Highlands and its shops, educational facilities, industrial estates and other commercial enterprises serve a huge hinterland. It is also a major tourist destination, the number of visitors swelling for the annual Highland Games held in Inverness. The town is divided by the River Ness and there is much to see on both sides of the river. The main shopping centre is to the east of the Ness. The Eastgate Centre is a large modern shopping complex but many historic buildings are also to be found amongst the network of streets surrounding the castle. The western bank enjoys a slower pace and it is here that some of the city's attractive parks can be explored as well as a world class leisure complex.

The East Bank
Visit Scotland, the tourist information centre is situated up a flight of steps on the High Street just below the castle.
Inverness Castle
The present castle is relatively modern but an earlier one on the same site was that of King Malcolm, built in 1057 after the death of the infamous MacBeth who had murdered Malcolm's father, King Duncan. Later kings also resided in Malcolm's castle and it was much fought over: In 1303 it was captured by the English King Edward I then later recaptured by Robert the Bruce. In 1455 it was taken over by the Lord of the Isles.
In 1562 Mary Queen of Scots was refused admission by the Governor of the castle and spent the night in a house on Bridge Street. The Governor was later executed for his impertinence.
Oliver Cromwell built a citadel in the town in 1652 and the remains of this and the castle were combined to become the first Fort George (the later one being sited out of Inverness.) In the 1745 uprising the castle was captured by the Jacobites but then quickly regained by the George II's Hanoverian army, only to be taken by Prince Charles the following

year and blown up to prevent the Hanoverians regaining control. The castle then lay mostly abandoned until 1834.
The present castle, designed by architect William Burn of Edinburgh, was built in 1836 to house a courthouse. A prison was then added in 1846.
Today, the castle is the home of Inverness Sheriff Court and many a photograph requires a good deal of editing to remove the prison vans from the front of the castle!
The Drum Tower is open to the public and there are excellent views of the city

Inverness Castle & The River

from the castle grounds. "**The Castle Garrison Encounter**" enables visitors to experience some of the aspects of life as an eighteenth century soldier.
A statue of Flora MacDonald is to be

found on the castle terrace. The heroine is looking out to the west and has done so from this point since 1899 when a large crowd gathered to see the unveiling of the statue.

Inverness Museum and Art Gallery (admission free) is situated on Castle Wynd. The museum is dedicated to the history of Inverness and the surrounding area, while the art gallery houses a changing programme of exhibitions. Nearby is an excellent cafe, renowned for its soup.

The Town House

The Town House is a magnificent Victorian Gothic style civic building, designed by Matthews and Lawrie and completed in 1882. It dominates the High Street from the bottom of Castle Street. The only cabinet meeting ever held outside London was called here by Lloyd George in 1921, as the King and various members of the cabinet

The Town House

were also north of the border. The "Inverness Formula" worked out at that meeting formed the basis for the treaty creating the Irish Free State. The building presently houses offices of the Highland Council but guided tours are available. In front of the building is the **Clach-na-Cuddlin** ("the stone of the tub") which is

thought to have possibly been the original coronation seat of the Macdonalds but which was used for many years as a stopping off point for women fetching water from the river and resting their buckets on the stone. Inside the building is a portrait of Flora Macdonald.

An interesting shop is **J. Graham and Co.** on Castle Street, who stock an extensive selection of high class clothing for Scottish outdoor pursuits. They also sell fishing tackle and can arrange for **salmon and trout fishing** as well as tuition in casting.

The Tollbooth Steeple

The Tollbooth Steeple

This impressive tower on Church Street was built in 1791. Three bronze bells hang in the 45m high tower. An earth tremor in 1816 damaged the tower which had to be repaired.

Abertarff House, also on Church Street, is the oldest surviving building in the city. It dates from 1593 and is owned by the National Trust for Scotland but is not open to the public. **Dunbar's Hospital** was built in 1668 as a hospital for the poor and as a grammar school. It was later used as a library but has since been converted into flats. At the junction of Friar's Lane and Church Street is the **Old Gaelic Church** which is now home to a second hand book shop and cafe. Nearby is the **Old High Church**, founded in the twelfth century as the parish church of St. Mary but the present building dates from

1772. As such it is the city's oldest church. Prisoners from the Battle of Culloden were executed in the graveyard here and some of the gravestones still bear the marks of musket balls.

The Victorian Market

The Victorian Market was built in 1870 and rebuilt after a fire in1890. It has entrances on all four surrounding streets and houses a fascinating selection of smaller shops. A model railway runs around part of the market above head height. The keystones above two of the entrances have animal carvings on them.

Market Interior

Falcon Square

Falcon Square is named after John Falconer. The elegant buildings which line one side of the square were originally part of an iron foundry owned by Mr. Falconer. Built in 1858 this had fallen into disrepair but was then dismantled, moved sixty yards and rebuilt as part of the Eastgate/city centre

Falcon Square

redevelopment. A forty feet high pillar stands in the square. Designed by local artist Gerald Laing, it is a modern representation of the Mercat Cross which once marked the centre of every Scottish town. The stone column is set on a granite plinth and has nine bronze sculptures which include a Scottish unicorn, four peregrine falcons in different stages of attacking prey and four sundials around the base.

The Eastgate Centre is the hub of

Noah's Ark clock, Eastgate Centre

Inverness shopping. Most of the major retail names are to be found here. A stunning bronze statue created by artist Leonie Gibbs forms a centre piece to the main hall. Entitled "The Falcon's Return," this is presumably also a subtle memorial to John Falconer. A firm favourite with children (and grown-ups too!) is the overhead **automaton clock** in the centre. Each hour a monkey emerges from Noah's ark to climb a tree to strike the hour on a bell.

Bellfield Park is one of the city's hidden gems, one of its smaller parks but one which is renowned for its spectacular floral displays. There is also tennis, bowling and a children's play area.

Ness Walk and **Ladies Bank** are the paths which run next to the river and past the imposing **War Memorial** on the east

Ladies' Walk

bank. A pleasant circular walk can combine this part of the east bank with the other bank of the river by crossing either via the pedestrian bridge or walking through the Ness Islands.

The War Memorial

Longman Drive (not to be confused with Longman Road) runs along the eastern bank of the river and is well worth a detour for the best views of the Kessock Bridge, as well as possible sightings of a large colony of bottle-nosed dolphins which inhabit the Moray Firth. **Dolphin spotting cruises** leave from Shore Street Quay.

It is a popular place for bird spotters all year round and there is a hide half way along. Keys are obtainable from the Highland Council service point on Church Street. **Inverness Yacht Marina** is also just off Longman Drive.

The Kessock Bridge

The Kessock Bridge

The Kessock Bridge is one of the iconic landmarks of Inverness and links North and South Kessock carrying the A9 across from Inverness to the Black Isle. It was completed in 1982 and is 1056m in length. It spans the narrowest part of the Moray Firth, where this then becomes the Beauly Firth

Hootananny, Church Street, features live music every night. Another popular city centre music venue is **The Iron Works**.

Scottish Showtime at the **Spectrum Theatre** near the bus station is a Scottish Evening staged for visitors on several nights a week during the summer months.

The Kilt Maker (Hector Russell) on Bridge Street is a "must visit." For a nominal fee visitors can learn all about the history of tartan and the kilt in two audio visual presentations and then watch actual kilts being made in the workshops.

Holm Mills Shopping Village is on the Dores road just outside the city centre. It has a variety of retail outlets for Scottish foods, tartans, whiskies and beers as well as an archive of clan histories where visitors can purchase their own clan certificate.

Churches along the river

One of the most noticeable features about the banks of the River Ness, on both sides, is the number of churches. Within a

Ness Bank Church

very short distance there are no less than nine which greatly add to the elegance of the overall appearance of this part of the city. It is not practical to attempt a detailed history of each here. However, there is an excellent leaflet available from Visit Scotland about these beautiful buildings and their history.

The Ness Islands

Ness Islands

Opposite Bute Park a series of pleasant wooded islands in the middle of the River Ness are accessible from both sides of the river via two Victorian pedestrian suspension bridges, The present bridges,

designed by William Dredge, were erected in 1853 to replace earlier ones which had been swept away in a flood in 1849. The islands are popular with visitors and residents alike.

The West Bank

A good way to explore the quieter, western side of the river is to hire a bike. **Monster Bike Cycle Hire** on canal road by Muirtown lock gates will deliver bikes to your accommodation. Tel: 01463 729500 or 07752 102700.

Inverness Cathedral

Inverness Cathedral

St. Andrew's Scottish Episcopal Cathedral enjoys an imposing setting on the western bank of the River Ness. Built of pink sandstone it was designed by architect Alexander Ross and is built in Gothic style. It was "completed" in 1869 but had originally been scheduled to have two spires crowning its two square towers. However, funds ran out before the plan was completed and so the towers remained without spires.

It is a beautiful church, with a huge stained glass west window in contrast to the series of tall narrow stained glass windows at the other end of the building. The sculptures carved in the stone pulpit and the carvings on the oak choir and alter screens are truly magnificent.

Eden Court Theatre is a modern theatre and cinema situated on the river bank next to the cathedral.

Eden Court Theatre

The Highland House of Fraser, on the western bank of the river across Ness Bridge, is a fascinating place. As well as being manufacturers of Highland Dress and boasting a **kilt maker visitor centre,** the adjoining retail outlet has a huge choice of Scottish souvenirs and giftware.

Tomnahurich Cemetery ("the hill of the yews") is an eighteenth century cemetery on the A82 Fort William road on the outskirts of the city. It is situated on an "esker," a glacial ridge formed from deposits left by melting glaciers. The strenuous walk to the top is rewarded by magnificent views over the city and beyond. There is also an interesting War Memorial at the top.

Bught Park is the site of most of the city's sports and recreational facilities including **Inverness Ice Centre** (curling, figure skating, ice hockey), **Inverness Leisure** (swimming, water flumes, wave pool, sports halls) and **Inverness Shinty Club.** It is also where Inverness Highland Games are held annually. The park also boasts a touring caravan site.

The Floral Hall & Gardens in Bught Park is a delightful place to spend a quiet hour or two. As well as sheltered outdoor

The Floral Hall

gardens, there are a series of hot-houses with exotic plants and cacti, a waterfall and fish pool. The entire complex is extremely child-friendly, featuring an outdoor Teddy Bears' Den and imaginative colouring sheets. The **coffee shop** offers a tempting array of goodies.

Whin Park

Whin Park

Whin Park is a delightful children's adventure park with a miniature railway and a boating lake. There are a variety of well maintained and fun creations to climb and ride on – including, unusually, a swing with a large bucket seat suitable for disabled children. There are plenty of sitting places dotted amongst the children's rides and this really has to be one of the nicest parks of its kind.

Public Toilets east of the river
Castle Wynd, Eastgate Centre, Inverness Station, Bellfield Park
Internet access
Clanlan internet cafe Baron Taylor Street, Inverness Bus Station Internet cafe
Public Toilets west of the river
Whin Park
Internet access
Grafiks Internet , Tomnahurich Street (west side of river over Ness Bridge)

Away from the centre.....
Muirtown locks and Muirtown Basin
The canal curves around the western outskirts of the town, via a dramatic series of locks at Muirtown and beneath a swing bridge there to enter the **Muirtown Basin**, a fascinating place where there is always something to see. The canal leaves the basin under a further swing bridge, on its way to join the Beauly Firth via the sea lock at Clachnaharry.
Clachnaharry (meaning "stone of repentance") on the north western outskirts of Inverness was once a fishing village and retains much of its original character with tiny fisherman's cottages and three narrow streets. Clachnaharry was the scene of the **Battle of Clachnaharry** when Clan Munro defeated Clan Mackintosh in 1454. The Munros were returning home after a cattle raid. They had to cross Mackintosh land

and a dispute arose over the amount of money they had to pay for crossing that land. Tempers flared and a full scale

Clachnaharry sea lock

battle developed. The remains of a monument above Clachnaharry commemorates the battle. The top of the monument, a forty feet high column, fell over after being struck by lightning in 1951.
A swing bridge carries the railway over the canal here and, for rail enthusiasts, **Clachnaharry Signal Box** is worth a photograph. The walk along the tow path/ sea wall to the sea lock is interesting with good views of the Kessock Bridge.
For a truly wonderful culinary experience **The Clachnaharry Inn,** a seventeenth century coaching inn with spectacular views over the Beauly Firth to Ben

The Clachnaharry Inn

Wyvis, is the place to be. The emphasis is on real ale and locally sourced food, the menu combining traditional dishes such as home made fish pie and Scottish stovies with an extensive first class restaurant menu. (A real foodies' paradise, this one!)

Exploring Loch Ness and the Caledonian Canal from Inverness

Caley Cruises, on Canal Road, provide one of the most relaxed ways to explore Loch Ness and the Caledonian Canal from Inverness. Their luxury motor cruisers are available for weekends or longer holidays. Full instruction is given so no previous boat handling experience is necessary. (Tel: 01463 236328) For those with less time to spare, **Jacobite Experience Loch Ness** (Tel: 01463 233999) offer tours from an hour to a day. For a really special occasion try an exclusive **champagne and buffet cruise** on the **Eilidh Catriona**. (prebookings only – parties up to eight persons.Tel: 07818 068155.)

Several companies offer day tours further afield from Inverness by car, minibus and coach. Details of these are available from the Visit Scotland Office in the High Street.

Hotels

Inverness is blessed with a great number of good hotels, too many to list in a guide book of this sort. However, the following are just some which are worthy of mention for various reasons:

The Waterside Hotel enjoys a lovely position along the banks of the River Ness. In addition to accommodation, the hotel serves food all day with an imaginative menu ranging from light meals and home baking to a full restaurant menu. **The Royal Highland Hotel** is an excellent choice for a central position, sitting at the entrance to the main station. For Art Deco fans, **The Drumossie Hotel** is a ten minute drive from the city centre and is set in nine acres of beautiful grounds.

For a real treat, five minutes' drive out of Inverness, along the A862 Beauly road, **The Bunchrew House Hotel** is a turreted fairy tale sitting right on the shores of the Beauly Firth – a seventeenth century mansion, complete with an oak panelled drawing room, log fires and some of the finest cuisine in Scotland. Bunchrew House "Celtic Sauce" is cuisine art in its highest form!

The Bunchrew House Hotel

There are innumerable places within easy visiting distance of Inverness – enough to fill another guide book. The following sections aim only to deal with a few of the major attractions to west and east of the city, along the Beauly and Moray Firths.

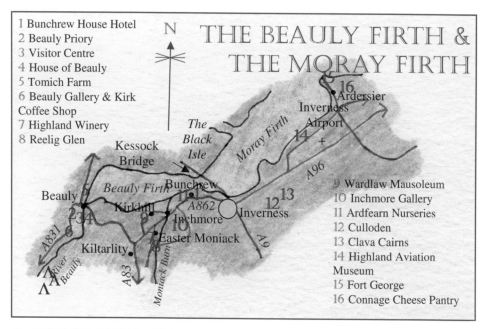

1 Bunchrew House Hotel
2 Beauly Priory
3 Visitor Centre
4 House of Beauly
5 Tomich Farm
6 Beauly Gallery & Kirk Coffee Shop
7 Highland Winery
8 Reelig Glen

9 Wardlaw Mausoleum
10 Inchmore Gallery
11 Ardfearn Nurseries
12 Culloden
13 Clava Cairns
14 Highland Aviation Museum
15 Fort George
16 Connage Cheese Pantry

THE BEAULY FIRTH & THE MORAY FIRTH

8. THE BEAULY FIRTH

The Beauly Firth is really an extension of the Moray Firth, being the stretch of water west of Inverness and the Kessock Bridge. On leaving Inverness the A862 runs close to the shoreline for several miles and this area is home to many species of wading birds. On a clear day there are open views across the Beauly Firth to Ben Wyvis and beyond to the mountains of Easter Ross. The only place of any size along this route is Beauly, where the River Beauly joins the Beauly Firth. There are several smaller places of interest but perhaps a logical way to cover this area is to travel west to Beauly and then make ones way back towards Inverness in a leisurely fashion. Depending on the time of day, The Bunchrew House Hotel (see previous page) makes an excellent stop for morning coffee, lunch or afternoon tea in the panelled drawing room.

Beauly

Beauly developed around the priory, the ruins of which dominate the village. In the days before there was a bridge over the River Beauly a ferry operated from here to Inverness. Some of the street names, such as Ferry Lane and Shore Street, still reflect this.The Lovatt Bridge, built in the early nineteenth century, was another of Telford's projects. Beauly is an attractive place with a large square at the centre. In the square are the remains of an ancient cross and a fountain dedicated to allied troops who were stationed at Beauly between 1939 and 1945. A series of river and country walks are signposted from the square, around the outside of which are some interesting and unique shops: **Alder Arts** is renowned in the art world for quality period Scottish paintings. They also offer a restoration service. Nearby is **award winning butcher** John M. Munro, famous for winning awards for locally produced Haggis, Black Pudding and Scottish Sausages. **"At the corner of the Square"** is the name of a tea room and delicatessen at that location. Opposite is the **Highland Tweed House** of Campbell and Co. For self caterers or anyone fancying a picnic, the bakery in the square is definitely recommended! The side streets leading off from the square are worthy of exploration. There are several antique and gift shops and the unusual Lovat Memorial Garden dedicated to Simon Fraser, a World War 2 hero.

Beauly Priory

Although ruined, the thirteenth century priory is still impressive. It was founded by monks of the French Valliscailian order and it is thought that the name Beauly may well come from the French "beau lieu" for "beautiful place" and which perhaps resulted from a comment made by Mary Queen of Scots when she visited the town in 1564. After the

Beauly Priory

Reformation the priory was no longer used and fell into disrepair, some of the stone being removed for use elsewhere. Part of the north transept was rebuilt in 1901 to serve as a mausoleum for the Mackenzie family.

Next to the priory is a visitor centre with **tourist information** and a craft shop.

The House of Beauly is a retail outlet selling a wide range of clothing, Scottish gifts etc. The food hall has a wide range of Scottish produce. (The cafe here serves excellent lunches.)

Tomich Farm, just outside Beauly on the Muir of Ord road, is an absolute delight. Budding mini farmers can drive the mini tractors and diggers in the giant sand pit or meet the friendly rare breed animals. The farm shop sells a wide range of local produce, including home reared free range pork and dry cured bacon.

The Priory Hotel, situated in the Square, offers real comfort in reasonably priced accommodation with a choice of menus from snack and bar menus to Scottish "high tea" or a full a la carte restaurant menu with the emphasis on Scottish dishes such as venison and scotch beef. (It is refreshing to discover a hotel where food is available at any time of the day.)

The Lovat Arms Hotel, owned by the Fraser family, also offers a typically Scottish welcome with log fires, malt whiskies and cuisine created from produce which would struggle to be more "local" – the farm being owned by the same people as the hotel. The hotel is pleased to arrange **hunting, shooting** or **salmon fishing** or fishing for trout on its privately owned loch just eleven miles from the hotel. **Clay pigeon shooting** is also available and tuition in any of the activities can be arranged with prior notice.

Beauly Gallery (seasonal) is a mile south of Beauly on the A831 Glen Affric road.

The gallery has a range of high class glassware, paintings, silverware, clothing, jewellery and children's toys. The adjoining **Kirk Coffee Shop** offers a wide range of cakes and pastries, coffees and herbal teas.

Approximately six miles west of Inverness (signposted from the A862) is **Moniack Castle**, home of the **Highland Winery**. This is a real "must visit!" The castle dates from around 1580 and the Fraser family carry on the tradition of making wines and preserves from wildflowers, fruit and tree sap. The result is an unusual range of country style wines and liqueurs as well as exquisite preserves and pickles. (Transform cold meats or sausage with a splash of Inverness sauce and say "goodbye for ever" to mint sauce once you've tried Moniack mint jelly!) **Reelig Glen,** close to the highland Winery, is of mixed woodland and includes a collection of old Douglas firs known as

Highland Winery

the Tall Trees Walk, several of which are over one hundred and seventy feet high. One, at over two hundred feet high, is officially the **tallest tree in Britain**. They were planted over a hundred years ago by James Baillie Fraser, the then owner of the land. The **Moniack Burn** runs through the woods which were given to

the Forestry Commission by Charles Ian Fraser of Reelig in 1949. There is a car park, picnic tables, several way marked trails (including wheelchair accessible routes,) with informative tree identification plaques, a nineteenth century stone bridge and a grotto.

The Wardlaw Mausoleum in the village of **Kirkhill** makes an interesting detour

Wardlaw Mausoleum

off the main A862. Restored in 1998, the mausoleum is an impressive building which houses the remains of four chiefs of the Lovat Fraser Clan. The main building dates from 1634, although the quirky belfry is from the eighteenth century. The mausoleum had originally been built onto the end of the old thirteenth century Wardlaw Church, now no longer there. The restoration involved reproducing mortar and lime wash to match as near as possible the original building materials. Visitors wishing to see the interior may obtain the key from either Pilgrim Cottage or the house called Rochelle next to the mausoleum. Kirkhill is signposted from the A862.

Inchmore Gallery, situated in an old church at Inchmore six miles west of Inverness, is an exciting and stimulating studio and gallery showcasing the work of modern Scottish artists and open Wednesday to Saturday throughout most of the year. At Bunchrew is **Ardfearn** **Nurseries**, well known for stocking a large range of trees, shrubs, herbaceous and alpine plants. There is also an on site florist and gift shop.

9. THE MORAY FIRTH

At the Kessock Bridge the Beauly Firth becomes the Moray Firth, widening out beyond Fortrose on the northern bank and Fort George on the southern bank to become a vast expanse of water which joins the North Sea. The Moray Firth is famous for its bird and other wildlife, but especially for the group of approximately a hundred bottlenose dolphins which live here, probably the most northerly group in the World. The A96 leaves Inverness and heads east towards Nairn and beyond to Forres and Elgin. However, within easy driving distance of Inverness are several places of interest.

Culloden

The Battle of Culloden, fought on Culloden Moor on April 16th 1746, was the last battle to be fought on British soil. The Jacobites, led by Charles Edward Stewart and supported by many Highlanders, were defeated by the

Culloden Visitor Centre

Government troops of George II. The outcome of the battle was inevitable: The Jacobites were disadvantaged in many ways, including their inferior numbers and the choice of battleground. The Highlanders were easy prey for the Government artillery and were largely mown down before they ever got close enough to use their swords. What resulted was a massacre: Over 1200 Jacobites were slain and another 3500 taken prisoner, some to be executed, some to be transported and many more "banished." The precise fate of several hundred of these men is not known. The **battlefield** has been cleared of woodland and restored to how it would have been at the time. Walking on the site of the battle can be a very moving experience. An exciting modern **Visitor Centre** brings the history of Culloden alive in an imaginative way, with models, the latest audio visual presentations, viewing areas and guides in Highland dress to add to the atmosphere. Facilities include a large restaurant and gift shop. There are several wells on or near the battlefield. **St Mary's Well** is said to be haunted by the ghosts of Highlanders. In **Culloden Woods i**s a well near which people often hang coloured rags as offerings in the hope of a cure for various ills.

Clava Cairns, a mile to the south east of Culloden at Balnuaran, is a set of three, well preserved prehistoric burial chambers, each surrounded by a ring of

Clava Cairns

standing stones. Some of the stones bear mysterious "cup marks." The cairns date from around 2000BC. There is a small car park next to the site.

Railway Viaduct - From the car park for the cairns there are excellent views of an impressive but more modern structure – an elegant, many-arched railway viaduct.

The Highland Aviation Museum is a small but fascinating museum accessed from the industrial estate at the side of Inverness Airport. Open at weekends, it is a real "find" for aviation enthusiasts with noses of various iconic aircraft, including a rare Valiant.

Fort George is another "must visit" destination and one where there is so much to see and do that it is easy to spend an entire day here. Seven miles from the A96, it is a massive fort built on a headland jutting out into the Moray Firth. Originally completed in 1769, some twenty years after its inception, it still houses a

Fort George

barracks today. Sitting behind huge grassed fortifications and amongst enormous ditches or "ravines," it is easy to appreciate how impregnable the fort was. (Entrance to the fort is by drawbridge!) There are several interesting displays and exhibitions, including reconstructions of barrack rooms and the powder magazine. The **regimental museum** is fascinating, some of the prized exhibits being arms of the Seafield Collection. From over a mile of ramparts there are stunning views over the Moray Firth.

One particularly user-friendly feature at Fort George is the availability of well serviced and fully charged motorised scooters for the disabled, robust enough to cope with the slope up to the ramparts! An excellent and spotlessly clean cafe serves really good food, including a "roll and roast" – chunky slices of Scotch beef with gravy in a bread roll. (Definitely recommended by the author and her Dad!) A gift shop sells a nice range of unusual souvenirs.

Ardersier

The road to the fort passes through the village of Ardersier which is interesting in its own right. It is a quirky place with some very old cottages. There are picnic tables in a pleasant situation by the water's edge. Nearby is **Connage Cheese Pantry** where it is possible for visitors to watch cheese being made. Above the village is a viewpoint which affords panoramic views of the Moray Firth.

Public Toilets
The Square, Beauly

USEFUL INFORMATION

Please note: The majority of services which may be required by visitors to Inverness are readily available in the city and therefore not necessarily listed below.

Telephone numbers

Police (emergency) 999
Ardersier: 01667 462222
Beauly: 01463 782222
Culloden: 01463 794550
Drumnadrochit: 01456 450222
Fort Augustus: 01320 366222
Fire (emergency) 999
Ambulance (emergency) 999
Coastguard (emergency) 999
Mountain Rescue (emergency) 999
Hospitals
Inverness Raigmore 01463 704000
NHS 24 08454 242424
Pharmacy
Beauly: L.Lawson 01463 782241
Drumnadrochit: Great Glen
Pharmacy 01456 450838
Visit Scotland Tourist Information Centres can be found at:
Drumnadrochit - the main car park
Inverness - Castle Wynd
Bus Companies
City Link: 08705 505050
National Express: 0870 5808080
Trains
National Rail Enquiries 08457 484950
Breakdown recovery
Fort Augustus, West End Garage. 01320 366247

Taxis
Beauly (Beauly Taxis) 01463 782498
Beauly (Inverness Airport Taxis) 01463 783763
Drumnadrochit (Drumnadrochit Private Hire) 01456 450617
Invergarry (Great Glen Travel) 01809 501222
Fort Augustus (West End Garage) 013210 366247

Ordnance Survey Maps

Road Map 1 Northern Scotland, Orkney & Shetland. Scale: 1: 250,000
Landranger Series. Scale: 1: 50,000
26 Inverness & Loch Ness
27 Nairn & Forres
34 Fort Augustus
35 Kingussie & The Monadhliath Mountains
Explorer Series. Scale: 1: 25,000
400 Loch Lochy & Glen Roy
415 Glen Affric & Glen Moriston
416 (side1) Inverness, Loch Ness & Culloden (side 2)
Fort Augustus 417 Monadhliath Mountains North & Strathdearn
422 Nairn & Cawdor

Bibliography:

Beyond The Great Glen: F. Reid Corson
The Glory of Scotland: J.J.Bell
A Country Called Stratherrrick: Alan B. Lawson
New Ways Through The Glens: A .R .B. Haldane

"SEE IT.... DO IT.... DON'T MISS IT !"

Visit our website:
www.scotlandguidebooks.co.uk

64